THE
ANATOMY
OF
POWER

THE
ANATOMY
OF
POWER

John Kenneth Galbraith

Houghton Mifflin Company Boston

Library of Congress Cataloging in Publication Data

Galbraith, John Kenneth, date
The anatomy of power.

Includes bibliographical references and index.
1. Power (Social sciences)   I. Title.
HM271.G27   1983   303.3   83-12622
ISBN 0-395-34400-X
ISBN 0-395-38170-3 (pbk.)

Printed in the United States of America

V 10 9 8 7 6 5 4 3 2 1

Houghton Mifflin Company paperback, 1985

FOR MARCIA LEGRU AND AUSTIN OLNEY
to whose conditioned and compensatory power
I have been happily subservient
for these many years

A Word of Thanks

As usual, I am in the debt of loyal and much-loved friends. One is Edith Tucker, a diversely talented community leader in Wellesley, Massachusetts, who combined an infinity of other duties with the typing and retyping of my drafts and highly pertinent criticism of whatever seemed incomplete or obscure. Ann Livingston shared in the typing, helped on the research and checking, and most adeptly managed and suppressed the annoyances of life so that I could keep my thoughts fairly continuously on the book. Most of all, I am indebted to Andrea Williams, my partner in this effort as in so many before, who, in a just world, would be listed, if not as the fellow author, then as the most talented of editors.

Contents

Contents

Foreword

FOR SOME FORTY YEARS, more years than I like to think, I have been involved with the subject of power — with the ideas and, in some degree, the practice. During World War II, as the person in charge of price control, I was thought to be at the center of power, a location that conveyed an impression of greater authority to others than it did to me. At other times in other positions I have been on the margins, better situated to observe than to have influence. As to writing, my first book was subtitled *The Concept of Countervailing Power*; I there argued that an opposing exercise of power is the principal solvent of economic power, the basic defense against its exercise in economic affairs. I returned to power as the central theme of *The New Industrial State*, which, not quite alone, I consider my principal effort in economic argument. My presidential address for the American Economic Association a decade ago was on "Power and the Useful Economist"; in it I contended that economics divorced from consideration of the exercise of power is without meaning and certainly without relevance. I have recurred to the concept less formally a dozen times, maybe more. I have rarely encountered an article or treatise on the subject without looking to see how it was handled — if, in useful result, at all. This book — I thought once of calling it an extended essay — is what I have learned from experience, reading, writing, and associated effort at understanding. My claim is not to the whole subject but to what I have learned about it.

I have become persuaded over the years of the common factors that lie behind the usual references to economic, political, military, and religious power and that include the power attributed to the press, television, and public opinion. These everyday references, since they do not indicate the underlying constants, regularly conceal as much as or more than they reveal. I have been concerned to make wholly visible these constants — to identify the sources of power in personality, property, and organization and to see the instruments by which power is exercised and enforced. I hope, as one result, that my readers will henceforth have a more explicit sense of what that word embraces and what it implies in the particular economic, political, or other matter under discussion.

As I have written on power, so I have read on it, and that reading has become a part of the inventory on which I have here drawn. I believe that some of my indebtedness is reasonably evident — to Max Weber, to Bertrand Russell, and to Adolf A. Berle, Jr., the diversely talented Roosevelt brain truster, diplomat, lawyer, and writer on social, political, and economic issues. It was Berle who, more than anyone else, encouraged my interest in the subject. I also owe much to C. Wright Mills's classic *The Power Elite*, to Charles S. Lindblom's *Politics and Markets*, to the varied economic writings of my friend Wallace C. Peterson, and to such interesting recent books as Richard Sennett's *Authority* and Dennis Wrong's *Power*. And to more. Like others, I am not always sure of the sometimes distant source of ideas I have accumulated; I am slightly more certain about the ideas I do not find useful. I suppose, for example, that I have been influenced by Machiavelli, but I have long suspected what Max Lerner has suggested, that he is most frequently cited by people who have not read him.

In telling of a lifelong interest in the subject of power, I must not seem to suggest, even remotely, that I have read all that has been written on it. No life is that long; there are some books that simply cannot be read; and there is much, I am sure, that I have missed. Everyone should be very cautious in his claims where the literature on power is concerned.

There is a tendency on the part of those who write on power, including quite a few who write out of wide-ranging knowledge and intelligence, to allow the subject to drag them into dense complexity and deep subjectivity. One can understand the temptation: complexity and subjectivity are a protection against critics who can be said to have missed the point; they are even more serviceable as an alternative to the toil and frustration of difficult clarification. But they are also a disguise for truth — a substitute for a clear, stark view of essentials. I have tried for such a view — I have sought to keep the sources and instruments of power constantly before the eyes of the reader. Partly for this reason, and partly for want of competence, I have side-stepped some issues, most notably, as I later tell, the role of the courts in the regulation of power. Also, I haven't hesitated to repeat what serves my argument or illustration. I would be sorry were such reiteration thought inadvertent or, anyhow, always so. I have wanted to be sure that, the covering flesh having been stripped away, the anatomy of power stands fully revealed.

THE
ANATOMY
OF
POWER

I

The Anatomy of Power

An Overview

The subject [is] not . . . remote, philosophical, or esoteric.
— ADOLF A. BERLE, JR.
Power

FEW WORDS are used so frequently with so little seeming
need to reflect on their meaning as power, and so it has
been for all the ages of man. In association with kingship
and glory it was included in the ultimate scriptural acco-
lade to the Supreme Being; millions still offer it every day.
Bertrand Russell was led to the thought that power, along
with glory, remains the highest aspiration and the greatest
reward of humankind.[1]

Not many get through a conversation without a reference to power. Presidents or prime ministers are said to
have it or to lack it in the requisite amount. Other politicians
are thought to be gaining in power or losing it. Corporations
and trade unions are said to be powerful, and multinational
corporations dangerously so. Newspaper publishers, the
heads of the broadcasting networks, and the more articulate, uninhibited, intelligent, or notorious of their editors,

[1] "Of the infinite desires of man, the chief are the desires for power
and glory." *Power: A New Social Analysis* (New York: W. W. Norton,
1938), p. 11.

I

columnists, and commentators are the powers that be. The Reverend Billy Sunday is remembered as a powerful voice; the Reverend Billy Graham is now so described. So is the Reverend Jerry Falwell; indeed, such has been his seeming power as a moral leader that he has been thought by some to be giving morality a bad name.

The references continue. The United States is a large and otherwise important country; so is the Soviet Union. But it is their power that evokes the common notice; they are the great powers, or the superpowers. Britain, once also a great power, is no longer powerful. All know that in recent times the United States has been losing some of its industrial power to Germany and Japan. None of these and the myriad other references to power is ever thought to require explanation. However diversely the word is used, the reader or listener is assumed to know what is meant.

And doubtless most do — to a point. Max Weber, the German sociologist and political scientist (1864–1920), while deeply fascinated by the complexity of the subject, contented himself with a definition close to everyday understanding: power is "the possibility of imposing one's will upon the behavior of other persons."[2] This, almost certainly, is the common perception; someone or some group is imposing its will and purpose or purposes on others, including on those who are reluctant or adverse. The greater the capacity so to impose such will and achieve the related purpose, the greater the power. It is because power has such a commonsense meaning that it is used so often with so little seeming need for definition.

[2] *Max Weber on Law in Economy and Society* (Cambridge: Harvard University Press, 1954), p. 323. See Reinhard Bendix, *Max Weber: An Intellectual Portrait* (Garden City, N.Y.: Doubleday, 1960), pp. 294–300. Elsewhere Weber said of power that it is the ability of one or more persons to "realize their own will in a communal act against the will of others who are participating in the same act."

But little more about power is so simple. Unmentioned in nearly all references to it is the highly interesting question as to how the will is imposed, how the acquiescence of others is achieved. Is it the threat of physical punishment, the promise of pecuniary reward, the exercise of persuasion, or some other, deeper force that causes the person or persons subject to the exercise of power to abandon their own preferences and to accept those of others? In any meaningful reference to power, this should be known. And one should also know the sources of power — what it is that differentiates those who exercise it from those who are subject to the authority of others. By what license do some have the right, whether in large matters or small, to rule? And what causes others to be ruled? It is these questions — how power is enforced, what accords access to the methods of enforcement — that this book addresses.

2

The instruments by which power is exercised and the sources of the right to such exercise are interrelated in complex fashion. Some use of power depends on its being concealed — on their submission not being evident to those who render it. And in modern industrial society both the instruments for subordinating some people to the will of others and the sources of this ability are subject to rapid change. Much of what is believed about the exercise of power, deriving as it does from what was true in the past, is obsolete or obsolescent in the present.

Nonetheless, as Adolf Berle observed, the subject is not a remote or esoteric thing. No one should venture into it with the feeling that it is a mystery that only the privileged can penetrate. There is a form of scholarship that seeks

3

not to extend knowledge but to exclude the unknowing. One should not surrender to it and certainly not on a subject of such great practical importance as this. All conclusions on power can be tested against generally acceptable historical evidence and most of them against everyday observation and uncomplicated common sense. It will help, however, to have the basic facts of power in mind at the outset and thus to proceed with a clear view of its essential character — its anatomy.

3

Power yields strongly, in a secular way, to the rule of three. There are three instruments for wielding or enforcing it. And there are three institutions or traits that accord the right to its use.

It is a measure of how slightly the subject of power has been analyzed that the three reasonably obvious instruments of its exercise do not have generally accepted names. These must be provided: I shall speak of condign, compensatory, and conditioned power.

Condign power wins submission by the ability to impose an alternative to the preferences of the individual or group that is sufficiently unpleasant or painful so that these preferences are abandoned. There is an overtone of punishment in the term, and this conveys the appropriate impression.[3] It was the undoubted preference of the galley slave

---

[3] I have taken some liberties in the selection and use of this term. According to strict dictionary usage, *condign* has an adjectival relationship to *punishment*. A condign punishment is, broadly speaking, an appropriate or fitting one. Were one scrupulously pedantic, the reference here and throughout would be to *condign punishment*. I omit the latter word with the thought, first articulated by Lewis Carroll, that one can have a word mean what one chooses it to mean

to avoid his toil, but his prospective discomfort from the lash for any malingering at the oars was sufficiently unpleasant to ensure the requisite, if also painful, effort. At a less formidable level, the individual refrains from speaking his or her mind and accepts the view of another because the expected rebuke is otherwise too harsh.

Condign power wins submission by inflicting or threatening appropriately adverse consequences. Compensatory power, in contrast, wins submission by the offer of affirmative reward — by the giving of something of value to the individual so submitting. In an earlier stage of economic development, as still in elementary rural economies, the compensation took varied forms — including payments in kind and the right to work a plot of land or to share in the product of the landlord's fields. And as personal or public rebuke is a form of condign power, so praise is a form of compensatory power. However, in the modern economy, the most important expression of compensatory power is, of course, pecuniary reward — the payment of money for services rendered, which is to say for submission to the economic or personal purposes of others. On occasion, where reference to pecuniary payment conveys a more exact meaning, this term will be used.

It is a common feature of both condign and compensatory power that the individual submitting is aware of his or her submission — in the one case compelled and in the other for reward. Conditioned power, in contrast, is exercised by changing belief. Persuasion, education, or the

---

— "neither more nor less." A tempting alternative would have been "coercive" power as used by Dennis H. Wrong in *Power: Its Forms, Bases and Uses* (New York: Harper Colophon Books, 1980). His discussion of coercive authority (pp. 41–44) parallels in a general way my use of *condign power*. However, it less specifically implies the instrument to which the individual (or group) surrenders, that which brings the submission.

social commitment to what seems natural, proper, or right causes the individual to submit to the will of another or of others. The submission reflects the preferred course; the fact of submission is not recognized. Conditioned power, more than condign or compensatory power, is central, as we shall see, to the functioning of the modern economy and polity, and in capitalist and socialist countries alike.

4

Behind these three instruments for the exercise of power lie the three sources of power — the attributes or institutions that differentiate those who wield power from those who submit to it. These three sources are personality, property (which, of course, includes disposable income), and organization.

Personality — leadership in the common reference — is the quality of physique, mind, speech, moral certainty, or other personal trait that gives access to one or more of the instruments of power. In primitive societies this access was through physical strength to condign power; it is a source of power still retained in some households or youthful communities by the larger, more muscular male. However, personality in modern times has its primary association with conditioned power — with the ability to persuade or create belief.

Property or wealth accords an aspect of authority, a certainty of purpose, and this can invite conditioned submission. But its principal association, quite obviously, is with compensatory power. Property — income — provides the wherewithal to purchase submission.

Organization, the most important source of power in modern societies, has its foremost relationship with conditioned power. It is taken for granted that when an exercise of power is sought or needed, organization is required. From the organization, then, come the requisite persuasion and the resulting submission to the purposes of the organization. But organization, as in the case of the state, also has access to condign power — to diverse forms of punishment. And organized groups have greater or lesser access to compensatory power through the property of which they are possessed.

This brings up a final point. As there is a primary but not exclusive association between each of the three instruments by which power is exercised and one of the sources, so there are also numerous combinations of the sources of power and the related instruments. Personality, property, and organization are combined in various strengths. From this comes a varying combination of instruments for the enforcement of power. The isolation or disentangling of the sources and instruments in any particular exercise of power, the assessment of their relative importance, and the consideration of the changes in relative importance over time are the task of this book.

In earliest Christian days, power originated with the compelling personality of the Savior. Almost immediately an organization, the Apostles, came into being, and in time the Church as an organization became the most influential and durable in all the world. Not the least of its sources of power was its property and the income thus disposed. From the combination of personality (those of the Heavenly Presence and a long line of religious leaders), the property, and, above all, the unique organization came the conditioned belief, the benefices or compensation, and the threat of condign punishment either in this world or the next that, in the aggregate, constituted the religious power. Such is the complex of factors incorporated in and, in great measure, concealed by that term. Political power, economic power, corporate power, military power, and other such references similarly and deeply conceal an equally diverse interrelationship. When they are mentioned, their inner nature is not pursued.[4] My present concern is with what is so often kept hidden.

We will look first at the instruments by which power is exercised and then at the sources. Thereafter we shall come to the way power has developed over time and its reality in our own day. But before that, it is necessary to have a word on the purposes for which people seek power and also on the mood in which one approaches the subject.

5

As with much concerning power, the purposes for which it is sought are widely sensed but more rarely articulated. Individuals and groups seek power to advance their own interests, including, notably, their own pecuniary interest. And to extend to others their personal, religious, or social values. And to win support for their economic or other social perception of the public good. The businessman buys the submission of his workers to serve his economic purposes — to make money. The religious leader persuades his congregation or his radio or television audience because he thinks his beliefs should be theirs. The politician seeks the support, which is to say the submission, of voters so that he may remain in office. Preferring clean to dirty air, the

[4] As others have held. "Perhaps no subject in the entire range of the social sciences is more important, and at the same time so seriously neglected, as the role of power in economic life." Melville J. Ulmer, "Economic Power and Vested Interests," in *Power in Economics*, edited by K. W. Rothschild (Harmondsworth, Eng.: Penguin Books, 1971), p. 245.

conservationist seeks to enforce respect for his preference on those who make automobiles or own factories. The latter seek submission to their own desire for lower costs and less regulation. Conservatives seek submission to their view of the economic and social order and the associated action; liberals or socialists seek similar submission to theirs. In all cases, as will sufficiently be noted in ensuing chapters, organization — the coming together of those with similar interests, values, or perceptions — is integral to the winning of such submission, to the pursuit of power.

Everyday language comments regularly on the reasons for which power is being pursued. If it is narrowly confined to the interest of an individual or group, one says it is being sought for selfish ends; if it reflects the interest or perception of a much larger number of people, those involved are thought inspired leaders or statesmen.

It is also recognized that the purposes for which power is being sought will often be extensively and thoughtfully hidden by artful misstatement. The politician who seeks office on behalf of the pecuniary interests of affluent supporters will be especially eloquent in describing himself as a public benefactor, even a diligent and devoted friend of the poor. The adequately educated businessman no longer employs workers to enhance his profit; his deeper purpose is to provide employment, advance community well-being, and ensure the success of the free enterprise system. The more fervent evangelist is overtly concerned with the salvation of sinners, bringing the unrighteous to grace; anciently he has been known to have his eye on the collection plate. A deeply ingrained and exceedingly valuable cynicism is the appropriate and frequent response to all avowals of the purposes of power; it is expressed in the omnipresent question, "What is he really after?"

Much less appreciated is the extent to which the purpose

of power is the exercise of power itself.[5] In all societies, from the most primitive to the ostensibly most civilized, the exercise of power is profoundly enjoyed. Elaborate rituals of obeisance — admiring multitudes, applauded speeches, precedence at dinners and banquets, a place in the motorcade, access to the corporate jet, the military salute — celebrate the possession of power. These rituals are greatly rewarding; so are the pleas and intercessions of those who seek to influence others in the exercise of power; and so, of course, are the acts of exercise — the instructions to subordinates, the military commands, the conveying of court decisions, the statement at the end of the meeting when the person in charge says, "Well, this is what we'll do." A sense of self-actuated worth derives from both the context and the exercise of power. On no other aspect of human existence is vanity so much at risk; in William Hazlitt's words, "The love of power is the love of ourselves." It follows that power is pursued not only for the service it renders to personal interests, values, or social perceptions but also for its own sake, for the emotional and material rewards inherent in its possession and exercise.

However, that power is thus wanted for its own sake cannot, as a matter of basic decency, be too flagrantly conceded. It is accepted that an individual can seek power to impose his moral values on others, or to further a vision of social virtue, or to make money. And, as noted, it is permissible to disguise one purpose with another — self-

[5] "The healthy individual who gains power loves it." Dr. Harvey Rich (a Washington, D.C., psychoanalyst, quoted in the *New York Times*, November 9, 1982. Bertrand de Jouvenel puts the matter more vividly: "The leader of any group of men . . . feels thereby an almost physical enlargement of himself . . . Command is a mountain top. The air breathed there is different, and the perspectives seen there are different, from those of the valley of obedience." (*On Power: Its Nature and the History of Its Growth* [New York: Viking Press, 1949], p. 116.)

enrichment can be hidden behind great community service, sordid political intent behind a passionate avowal of devotion to the public good. But it is not permissible to seek power merely for the very great enjoyment that it accords.[6]

Yet while the pursuit of power for the sake of power cannot be admitted, the reality is, as ever, part of the public consciousness. Politicians are frequently described as "power-hungry"; the obvious implication is that they seek power to satisfy an appetite. Corporations take over other corporations not in pursuit of profits but in pursuit of the power that goes with the direction of a yet larger enterprise. This, too, is recognized. American politicians — senators, congressmen, cabinet officers, and Presidents — regularly sacrifice wealth, leisure, and much else to the rigors of public office. That the nonspecific exercise of power and the access to its rituals are part of the reason is fairly evident. Perhaps only from those so rewarded are the pleasures of power for its own sake extensively concealed.

6

A reference to power is rarely neutral; there are few words that produce such admiring or, in the frequent case, indignant response. A politician can be seen by some as a powerful and thus effective leader; seen by others, he is dangerously ruthless. Bureaucratic power is bad, but public servants with power to render effective public service are very good. Corporate power is dangerous; so, however, is a weakly administered enterprise. Unions in their exercise of power indispensably defend the rights of the workers;

[6] John F. Kennedy, a man of some candor in public expression, nearly did so. "I run for President," he said, "because that is where the action is." By *action* he was close to meaning power.

otherwise perceived, they are deeply in conflict with the liberty of their members and the well-being of employers and the public at large.

Much obviously depends on the point of view — on the differential responses arising from whose submission is being sought, whose ox is being gored. The politician who wins a tax reform of which one approves has engaged in a wise exercise of power; to those who must pay, it is or can be arbitrary, even unconscionable. The admiration for the exercise of power that wins a new airport is not shared by the people whose property abuts the landing strip.

The response to power is also, in substantial measure, a legacy of its past. Until nearly within living memory, black workers in the United States and white serfs in Imperial Russia were impelled to the will of the overseer, owner, or landlord by application of the whip. Power meant condign power of a particularly painful and sanguinary sort. The world has also had thousands of years of harsh experience with condign enforcement by military organization, an experience that is not yet at an end. It is this history and more that has given power its chilling name.

Further, as we shall see later in detail, much exercise of power depends on a social conditioning that seeks to conceal it. The young are taught that in a democracy all power resides in the people. And that in a free enterprise system all authority rests with the sovereign consumer operating through the impersonal mechanism of the market. Thus is hidden the public power of organization — of the Pentagon, the weapons firms, and other corporations and lobbyists. Similarly concealed by the mystique of the market and consumer sovereignty is the power of corporations to set or influence prices and costs, to suborn or subdue politicians, and to manipulate consumer response. But eventually it becomes apparent that organizations *do* influence government, bend it and therewith the people to their need and will. And that corporations are not subordinate to the market; instead the market that is supposed to regulate them is, in some measure, an instrument in their hands for setting their prices and incomes. All this being in conflict with social conditioning, it evokes indignation. Power thus concealed by social conditioning and then revealed seems deeply illegitimate.

Yet power, per se, is not a proper subject for indignation. The exercise of power, the submission of some to the will of others, is inevitable in modern society; nothing whatever is accomplished without it. It is a subject to be approached with a skeptical mind but not with one that has a fixation of evil. Power can be socially malign; it is also socially essential.[7] Judgment thereon must be rendered, but no general judgment applying to all power can possibly serve.

---

[7] "Power has two aspects . . . It is a social necessity . . . It is also a social menace." De Jouvenel, *On Power*, p. 283.

II

Condign and Compensatory Power

THE MOST DISTINCTIVE feature of both condign and compensatory power is their objectivity — or visibility. Those accepting the will of others are conscious of doing so; they are acting in consequence of a fairly deliberate calculation that this is the better course of action. It has become so because of the offer of some specific quid pro quo for their submission. Those exercising the power are also purposefully aware of what they are doing.

The difference between condign and compensatory power is the difference between negative and affirmative reward. Condign power threatens the individual with something physically or emotionally painful enough so that he forgoes pursuit of his own will or preference in order to avoid it. Compensatory power offers the individual a reward or payment sufficiently advantageous or agreeable so that he (or she) forgoes pursuit of his own preference to seek the reward instead. In less abstract language, condign power wins submission by the promise or reality of punishment; compensatory power wins submission by the promise or reality of benefit.

14

Condign power has an ancient and established relationship to physical punishment — to detention under variously uncomfortable conditions or to the inflicting of pain, mutilation, other imaginative torture, or death. This impression is not invalid; all societies recognize the unpleasant character of much condign punishment and the ease with which it verges on cruelty, and all have regulations controlling or presuming to control its use. Nothing so condemns a country or a system of government as promiscuous resort to its employment. However, the term condign power as here used has a broader connotation: it extends to power that is exercised by any form of adverse action or its threat, including fines, other property expropriation, verbal rebuke, and conspicuous condemnation by other individuals or the community.

2

Condign and compensatory exercises of power are both graduated to the urgency of the submission being sought or the extent, importance, or difficulty of that submission. Thus it is considered imperative in most societies that murder, rape, and other kinds of physical assault be prevented, that the would-be murderer or rapist be brought firmly into submission to the will of the community on these matters. These acts, accordingly, lie under a threat of heavier punishment than do minor theft or shoplifting, traffic violations, or casual breaches of the peace. Similarly, as regards compensatory power, it is assumed that the good worker or the one who works long hours will have a higher pecuniary reward than the less reliable performer. "I pay him well and I expect him to give his best to the job," which is to say a full submission to the will or purposes of the spokesman. Those involved in mental as opposed to physical effort or who carry the responsibilities of management are presumed to require a higher payment for their submission to the purposes of organization than those who render only physical or manual service, however adept or talented that may be.[1]

The proper gradation in condign punishment and compensatory reward is among the more disputed questions in modern society, the source of a very large amount of comment and contention. Is the punishment of the aforementioned murderer appropriate to the result sought? Or that of those guilty of treason? Is the penalty sufficient for those who do not submit to the public will on the use of marijuana, cocaine, or heroin? Are the salaries that bend executives to the purposes of the corporation excessive? Are they in keeping with the wages that win the services of those who work amidst the dirt and noise of the production line? Are those who serve public organization — who submit

[1] This is because there is a profound difference in the nature and extent of the submission that is made. The person on the shop floor or its equivalent gives more or less diligent and deft physical effort for a specified number of hours a day. Beyond that nothing in principle — not thought, certainly not conformity of speech or behavior — is expected. Of the high corporate executive a more complete submission to the purposes of the organization is usually required. He (or she) must speak and also think well of the aims of the enterprise; he may never in public and not wisely in private raise doubt as to the depth and sincerity of his own commitment. Many factors determine his large, often very large, compensation, including the need to pay for the years of preparation, for the considerable intelligence that is required, for the responsibility that is carried, and for the alleged risks of high position. As a practical matter, his rate of pay is also influenced by the significant and highly convenient role the executive plays in establishing it; much that accrues to the senior corporate executive is in response to his own inspired generosity. But there is also payment for the comprehensive submission of his individual personality to that of the corporation. It is no slight thing to give up one's self and self-expression to the collective personality of one's employer. Thus the high recompense. (Thus, also, the unique dullness of much corporate expression.) This is a matter to which I will return.

to the purposes of the state — paid enough or too much in comparison with their counterparts in private enterprise? What of soldiers whose submission is won partly by their pay, partly by the prospect of condign action if they show insufficient enthusiasm in the presence of the enemy, partly by a powerful social conditioning yet to be considered? The fascination with the subject of power lies in the number of windows it opens on everyday life. The concern in all societies for what is right or appropriate as to punishment or reward is one window through which we shall have frequent later occasion to look.

3

In all modern social attitudes a definite line is drawn between compensatory and condign power. Compensatory enforcement is thought to be far more civilized, greatly more consistent with the liberty and dignity of the individual, than condign enforcement. The position of the free laborer who works for pay is held to be in every way superior to that of the slave whose submission to the will and purposes of the master is encouraged by the sanguinary threat of physical punishment.

The difference is, indeed, great, but it should be attributed more to economic development than to social enlightenment. In the poor society the difference between condign and compensatory enforcement is small; only in the rich society does a major difference emerge. When poverty was general, free workers toiled in fear of the starvation and other privation that were the alternative to compensation. The slave worked out of fear of the lash. The preference for starvation as compared with a flogging could be a matter of taste. Thus, before the Civil War in the American South, the free worker was superior in social station to the black field hand. But he worked, nonetheless, under a threat of economic deprivation that may not have been greatly less compelling, on occasion, than the fears of the slave. Something could even be said, and, indeed, has been said, for the greater security of tenure of the slave. He could be beaten, but he could not be fired. It was with economic development that the two forms of enforcement strongly diverged. The free worker then acquired personal resources that would sustain him at least temporarily were he thrown out of work. Alternative employment opportunities became more numerous. Eventually there were unions. Unemployment compensation involved a notable shift away from the painful alternatives that united compensatory with condign enforcement. So work became ever more for the pecuniary reward, ever less because of the fears associated with loss of the job.

It may be noted in the American case that this divergence between the position of the bondsman and that of the free worker, in combination with the increasing ease of communication between the free states and the South, would eventually have made slavery economically impractical, much as it might still have been cherished by the plantation owners on moral, social, or traditional grounds.[2] The free worker's advantage being great and visible and transportation being available on the freight trains, defection to the North would have increased and become endemic. Recusant

[2] These are matters of especially enjoyed debate between historians. My former Harvard colleague Robert W. Fogel has been sharply criticized for holding that the position of the slave worker was not too greatly inferior to that of the free laborer in the antebellum years. (*Time on the Cross*. With Stanley L. Engerman. [Boston: Little, Brown, 1974]) I am content to concede that there is an economic as well as a moral difference between those positions and argue only that the difference increases, *pari passu*, with economic development itself.

owners, pocketing their principles, would have offered wage supplements to their slaves or, more likely, a share in the crop to stay faithful. Submission by the slave to the will of the master would, increasingly, have been because of compensatory reward rather than condign punishment. Such is the effect of economic development on the instruments of power. One could argue, though not wisely in respect to an event so greatly cherished in retrospect, that given the rate of economic growth in the last half of the last century, the Civil War would have been unnecessary, had it been delayed a couple of decades or so.

4

We have a useful glimpse here of the relationship between condign or compensatory power and what is called the work ethic. Work has always been thought peculiarly ethical for less well-paid workers in tedious employment; in the upper reaches of the social order, an imaginatively conceived use of leisure affirms a civilized tendency in those who indulge it. Welfare payments, unemployment compensation, and other forms of social insurance are thought to be especially damaging to the work ethic and thus to the poor. As such, they are a source of grave conservative indignation.

The conservative instinct is sound. Higher income and social welfare benefits do impair compulsion as a motivating force.[3] As the gap between condign and compensatory submission grows, so, accordingly, does concern for work habits. Complaints multiply as to the diligence of workers. Perhaps, some will conclude, a measure of deprivation or its threat

[3] "One puts up with employers who are inept, fools, or unpleasant if one wants to eat." Richard Sennett, *Authority* (New York: Knopf, 1980), p. 107. On this general point see Sennett's extended discussion in the same book, pp. 104 et seq.

is necessary to sustain discipline and the work ethic; this was an accepted tenet of the policy of the Reagan administration in the United States when it came to power in 1981. It is, however, necessary to ask whether a widening gap between condign and compensatory exercises of power in economic affairs is to be deplored. An economic system in which people work — submit to the will and purposes of others — in response to a generally affirmative reward rather than out of the negative compulsion caused by fear of the suffering from not doing so has something, many will think a great deal, to be said in its favor.

5

The abolition of slavery meant the withdrawal of the right of condign punishment to enforce toil, that is, to win submission to the will of the slave owner, and the substitution, however small, of compensatory reward. Owners of mills and mines once had the right of resort to physical violence or its threat to break strikes or otherwise bend recalcitrant workers to their will. This right also has been largely withdrawn, and its use, when it does occur now, is thought regressive. In Poland in the late autumn of 1981, the government resorted to martial law to prevent strikes and to win the submission of workers and students to the purposes of the state and the Communist party. Condign power, in effect, replaced compensatory power, the latter having been greatly weakened by a shortage of possible compensation in the form of food and other necessities. Needless to say, this reversion to condign power was much deplored.

At a more commonplace level, husbands originally won the submission or obedience of wives by the threat or frequent fact of condign assault. This is no longer well-regarded; the protection of battered wives has become a cause. The will of the schoolmaster was traditionally imposed by condign punishment; now to spare the rod is no longer to spoil the child. Preachers anciently won submission of their congregation to the faith they espoused by the promise that dissenters would face an exceptionally disagreeable punishment in the world hereafter. Now the hellfire-and-damnation preacher is often considered seriously archaic.

Along with the declining reputation of the condign exercise of power has gone an effort to minimize its severity where it does survive. In earlier times soldiers who deserted in the face of the enemy were subject to summary execution. In World War I, many were so dispatched. By World War II, this was no longer thought appropriate. Only one lone American was executed in that war for declining to brave enemy fire, and his case became a minor cause célèbre. The death penalty in most, though not quite all, modern societies has come to be regarded with disapproval. So also, of course, have torture, starvation, and flogging.

In hand with the decline in the reputation of condign power has gone a vigorous and extensive effort to broaden the effectiveness of compensatory power, especially for what are considered socially desirable purposes, most notably more intense economic effort and investment. A key word here is *incentive*; an incentive is something that makes more efficient and compelling the compensatory reward for socially desirable submission.[4] Few matters are more discussed by modern governments. Tax policy, monetary policy, farm policy, wage and labor policies, are all directly or indirectly concerned with the effect of a given action on incentives — on compensatory power. The relation of com-

[4] It has also come to suggest that someone is seeking more income for himself and is using social function as a cover.

pensation to effort is also a preoccupation of the large business enterprise, and it accounts for a major proportion of all formal economic discussion. Such is the current role of compensatory power.

Although the reputation and use of condign power have greatly declined in modern societies, and notably so in relation to compensatory power, its ancient aura survives. For those who once possessed the right to use it, it remains a factor in winning submission. The husband, parent, schoolmaster, policeman, sheriff, National Guardsman, and barroom bouncer all have authority now in consequence of a past association with condign power.

We see here, also, the basis of the conservative yearning for capital punishment, corporal punishment in schools, the dominance of men over women, more sanguinary powers for the police, enlarged rights of search and seizure, the right to promiscuous possession and, as necessary, use of lethal weapons. It is held that these relics of a generally more violent time are required for the defense of law and order or for otherwise winning acceptable social behavior. The more important reason is that all are manifestations of condign power. Such power was considerably more important in the past than it is now, and the natural business of conservatives is to conserve or retrieve from the past.

6

Central to both condign and compensatory power is the specific relationship between the reward offered or the punishment threatened and the submission achieved. The assembly-line worker would not stay long on the job in the absence of pay. He would not readily submit to overtime effort in the absence of overtime pay. The would-be criminal is deterred by the threat of the punishment to which he will be subject. The motorist observes the speed limit because of the fine to which he could be exposed.

But in all of these cases and others, another motive for submission is present: it is that submission reflects a proper, reputable, accepted, or decent form of behavior. Adults work partly because it is the thing to do. One should not waste life, idle away the time. In the inner sancta of the executive suite men (and the rare woman) are expected to give their total energies to the business enterprise; except when the case is being made for more pay or lower taxes, it would be insupportable for anyone there to suggest that executive effort is regulated in accordance with compensation, that high corporate officers looking at their salaries give less than their best. And the same is true in public affairs. No politician or important public official can be thought to be adjusting his effort to accord with his pay. Children obey their parents — submit to their will — because that is what children do. Some wives similarly submit to their husbands. And most people yield to public authority not from fear of condign punishment or hope of compensatory reward but because they are law-abiding citizens.

The problem of understanding power, as always, is the absence of pure cases. In intimate admixture with the condign or compensatory enforcement of power is the submission that comes because the individual believes or has been persuaded that this is somehow for him the better course. It is a submission that derives from belief. And such submission is not only of great but also of increasing importance. For as economic and social development have moved the society from condign physical enforcement to compensatory pecuniary reward, so they are now moving it toward an ever-increasing reliance on the use of conditioned power.

III

Conditioned Power

> . . . [T]he business of the world . . . consisteth almost in
> nothing else but a perpetual contention for honour, riches,
> and authority . . . [T]hese are indeed great difficulties, but
> not impossibilities; for by education, and discipline, they
> may be, and are sometimes reconciled.
> — THOMAS HOBBES
> *Leviathan*

> Textbook content shall promote citizenship and the under-
> standing of the free-enterprise system, emphasize patriotism
> and respect for recognized authority . . . Textbook content
> shall not encourage life-styles deviating from generally
> accepted standards of society.
> — Proclamation of the Texas
> State Board of Education, 1982

WHILE CONDIGN AND COMPENSATORY POWER are
visible and objective, conditioned power, in contrast, is subjective; neither those exercising it nor those subject to it
need always be aware that it is being exerted. The acceptance of authority, the submission to the will of others, becomes the higher preference of those submitting. This
preference can be deliberately cultivated — by persuasion
or education. This is explicit conditioning. Or it can be
dictated by the culture itself; the submission is considered
to be normal, proper, or traditionally correct. This is implicit
conditioning. No sharp line divides one from the other;

explicit conditioning shades by degrees into implicit.[1] In giving substance to these abstractions, I recur to the means by which men in the past, and considerably also in the present, have exerted power over women and bent them to their will.

Something in the exercise of masculine authority must be attributed to the superior access of the male to condign power — to the greater physical strength of a husband and its use to enforce his will on a physically weaker and insufficiently acquiescent spouse. And no one can doubt the frequent efficiency of compensatory power, of reward in the form of clothing, jewelry, equipage, housing, entertainment, and participation in social observances. These have long and adequately demonstrated their utility in securing feminine compliance with masculine will.

However, it will be evident on brief thought that male power and female submission have relied much more completely on the belief since ancient times that such submission is the natural order of things. Men might love, honor, and cherish; it was for long accepted that women should love, honor, and *obey*. Some of this was the product of specific education — of instruction at home, in the schools, and from the Church as to the proper role of women in the social order and in relation to the family. Until recently, courses in universities and colleges taught women but not men the homely arts — home economics and homemaking — with a strong implication that this was relevant to a normal submission to male will. Such implication in this form of instruction has not entirely disappeared.

But only a part of the subordination of women was

---

[1] For a perceptive treatment of what I here call conditioned power, see Charles E. Lindblom, *Politics and Markets: The World's Political-Economic Systems* (New York: Basic Books, 1977), especially pp. 52–62.

achieved by explicit instruction — explicit conditioning. Much and almost certainly more was (and is) achieved by the simple acceptance of what the community and culture have long thought right and virtuous or, in Max Weber's term, what is an established patrimonial relationship between ruler and ruled. This is implicit conditioning, a powerful force.

Overall, this conditioned submission of women proceeded from belief, belief that masculine will was preferable to undue assertion of their own and the counterpart belief by men that they were entitled by their sex or associated physical and mental qualities to dominate. A vast and greatly repetitive literature celebrated both this submission of women and the occasional remarkable or eccentric woman who, by personality, guile, or precise or extravagant use of sexual competence, managed to impose her will on community, government, lovers, or husbands.

There is proof of this power of belief in the nature of the modern effort at emancipation — the women's movement. Various forms of condign masculine power have been attacked, including the right of husbands to inflict physical or mental punishment. Relief from the compensatory power wielded by men has been sought through the development of employment opportunity for women outside the household and by publicizing the employment discrimination that keeps women in subordinate jobs. But a major part of the effort has been the challenge to belief — the belief that submission and subservience are normal, virtuous, and otherwise appropriate. The reiteration of such belief — insistence on what are called the traditional values of home, family, and religion — has, in turn, been central to the efforts and outcry of those, women perhaps more than men, who have resisted the move for emancipation.

2

As with the assertion of male dominance, so with other manifestations of power. The power of the Church, as earlier noted, was anciently supported by its access to condign punishment both in the present and in the world to come. And none would doubt the compensatory attraction of the benefices the Church bestowed. But overwhelmingly its power depended, as it still does, on belief. It is to the instilling and consolidating of belief that the Church has always, and wisely, devoted its major emphasis. So commonplace is this effort that the affirmations of belief have come to be thought identical with religion itself.

The case is the same with the military, as also already mentioned. Soldiers are and must be paid for their services. And a condign alternative is also frequently required for those who are reluctant to serve or to face the possibly mortal consequences of battle. But it has long been accepted that good soldiers are committed to the cause for which they are fighting — that willingness to accept death and dismemberment requires the high morale that proceeds from belief.[2] Mercenaries motivated only by compensatory

---

[2] Bertrand Russell, in a notable passage, supports this point: "It is easy to make out a case for the view that opinion is omnipotent, and that all other forms of power are derived from it. Armies are useless unless the soldiers believe in the cause for which they are fighting, or, in the case of mercenaries, have confidence in the ability of their commanders to lead them to victory. Law is impotent unless it is generally respected. Economic institutions depend upon respect for the law; consider, for example, what would happen to banking if the average citizen had no objection to forgery." *Power: A New Social Analysis* (New York: W. W. Norton, 1938), p. 136. Russell goes on to urge the importance of looking back to the sources of the opinion so emphasized.

power or raw conscripts motivated only by condign power have always been thought second-rate warriors.

Political leaders, to an unfortunate extent in much of the present-day world, still hold office because of their access to condign power — their ability to threaten confinement, torture, or the permanent dispatch of those who do not accept their will. Considerable use is still made by them of compensatory power, the ability to buy the support, that is, the subservience, of individuals who otherwise would not submit to authority. Forthright purchase of votes was commonplace in various parts of the United States until comparatively recent times. Similarly in other democracies. And in various forms — patronage, invitations to social observances, the conferral of honors, and notably the award of public contracts — compensatory power still persists. Again, however, as with religion and the military, conditioned power is far more important. Modern politicians devote themselves overwhelmingly to the cultivation of belief. In the democracies in the twentieth century political power consists in the largest measure of conditioned power. This also is a matter to which I will return.

Conditioned power is of great significance in economic life as well. The average worker responds to compensatory power; in its absence he would not work. But in all but the most tedious lines of endeavor he also has pride in his job and reflects in its performance what Thorstein Veblen called the instinct to workmanship. This instinct becomes increasingly important and increasingly avowed as one ascends in the corporate hierarchy. It is the pride of the senior executive (or the lesser aspirant) that he *really believes* in what he is doing. Executive compensation is still much cherished as a motivation; but the purposes of the business enterprise are deeply incorporated into belief and have an independent force. They are good and right, and belief in them is a highly effective manifestation of conditioned power.[3,4]

In all the familiar allusions to power, familial, religious, military, political, economic — references, it must be noted, that conceal as much as they reveal — the role of conditioned power is large. And it gets larger as an intimate aspect of all social development.

3

Conditioned power is the product of a continuum from objective, visible persuasion to what the individual in the social context has been brought to believe is inherently correct. As we have seen, such power can be explicit, the result of a direct and visible attempt to win the belief that, in turn, reflects the purposes of the individual or group seeking or exercising the power. Or the belief can be implicit in the social or cultural condition; submission to the authority of others reflects the accepted view of what the individual should do. As one moves from explicit to implicit conditioning, one passes from obtrusive, ostentatious effort to win belief to an imposed subordination that is unnoticed — taken for granted. And, an important point, the social acceptance of conditioned power rises steadily as one moves in this direction from explicit to implicit conditioning.

Thus one of the most explicit forms of conditioned power

---

[3] See p. 59.

[4] There is a very practical point here. Regularly it is argued in a far-from-disinterested way that more after-tax income is required to stimulate more effort and produce higher productivity. But, as we here see, it is conditioning, not compensation, that primarily induces the executive's subordination to corporate purpose. Given that that is so, there would be little or no added effort from any higher compensation, and in practice there isn't.

in modern industrial societies is exercised through advertising. By art and reiteration people are persuaded to *believe* in the peculiar conviviality associated with a particular brand of beer, the specific health-protecting qualities of a given brand of cigarettes, the high social acceptability that is associated with the whiteness of shirt collars, the unique moral tone of a particular politician, the desirability or unwisdom of a specific political initiative. In all cases the effect is the same; the buyer is brought to a belief in the purposes of the seller. He or she surrenders to the will of the purveyor of the beer, cigarettes, detergent, or political purpose. That this is not always perceived as an exercise of power does not make it less the case. That the belief may be shallow and the resulting subordination neither durable nor substantial does not alter the essential character of the effort. There are few manifestations of power in modern times that expend such costly and committed energy as the cultivation of belief and the resulting exercise of power through advertising.

However, partly because advertising is a wholly ostentatious attempt to capture belief, it is not a fully reputable way of winning it. It regularly invites its own resistance and disapproval. Accordingly, while a corporation seeking the subordination of consumers to the purchase of its products launches an advertising campaign, if it wishes to subordinate citizens to its political purposes — an escape from onerous regulation or allegedly unrighteous taxation — it launches an educational campaign. And so likewise any other group seeking submission to its public will. For winning belief, education, as compared with advertising, is socially far more reputable.

There are problems, however, with education. It also can, on occasion, be too overt. A politician can speak of informing his people; he cannot, without seeming to demean their intelligence, say they need education. A President can say in private that this or that is a matter on which people need instruction. When he goes on television, it is to tell them of what they as citizens should *be aware*. Press, television, and radio — collectively the media — are thought to have a large educational function. This they do not usually avow; their more tactful purpose is simply to *inform* their readers, viewers, or listeners.

That power is involved — that the submission of some to the purposes of others is being sought — is sufficiently indicated by the tension that surrounds access to the media. All recent Presidents of the United States have been recurrently at odds with television, press, and radio. That is partly because the media have a certain measure of control over the presidential access to conditioned power. And, additionally, the conditioning they seek may be in conflict with that sought by the President. Hence the conflict. Hence, also, the continuing presidential efforts, by no means unsuccessful, to seduce the press with personal attention, seeming confidences, fulsomely articulated flattery, social entertainments, grave deference, or other devices. And hence, finally, the much heralded and not unimportant brake imposed by the media on presidential power. One consequence is a substantially exaggerated view of the power of the press, radio, and television, a matter to which I will return in a later chapter.

4

No one is likely to question the importance of the explicit conditioning of the media as an instrument for winning submission and exercising power. Those so engaged are greatly and solemnly aware of their role. Less celebrated is the conditioning by formal education — by family, schools, colleges, and universities. All strongly cultivate the beliefs that allow of the exercise of power. Children in minimally competent schools are told from their earliest days that the authority of parents and teachers must be respected; that laws must be obeyed; that there is a presumption of wisdom in what a democratic government decides; that there is an acceptable code as regards property, dress, and personal hygiene; that the acceptance of leadership — the contented submission to the will of others — is a normal and commendable thing.[5] Part of the value that all educational institutions place on team sports lies in the training they provide in the largely automatic substitution of group or team goals for those of the individual, of the authority of the coach or captain for the team member's personal preference or thought.

Educational conditioning also wins the acceptance of very specific forms of power. Schools in all countries inculcate the principles of patriotism by such traditional folk rites as the recitation of a pledge of allegiance in the presence of the flag, by emphasis on heroic episodes from the past, and by direct instruction in the present value of military preparedness and achievement. This, in turn, is of high importance for winning acceptance of the related purposes of the state. The conditioning that requires all to rally around the flag is of particular importance in winning subordination to military and foreign policy. Its effect is to place questions of national security and national defense above partisan or other parochial challenge.

Educational conditioning extends also to the economic and social system. Children in Communist countries hear

[5] For a typically strong statement on this tendency, see C. Wright Mills, *The Power Elite* (New York: Oxford University Press, 1956), pp. 319–20.

relentlessly of the virtues of socialism, the need for full, enthusiastic submission to its purposes. But, except in degree, this effort is not peculiar to Communist education. Children in the United States hear in similar fashion of the virtues of free enterprise; there is a continuing demand from corporations and business organizations that the socialist example be emulated and there be more such instruction in schools and universities as well as for the public at large. To the extent that such instruction succeeds, those so educated are led to accept the purposes of the business world as valid expressions of the public and their own personal good. The seriousness with which this conditioning in schools is taken is attested by the furor that can still arise if adolescents are thought to have access in their libraries to books critical of, or otherwise in conflict with, socially acceptable views on the existing economic or social order.

The importance of direct educational conditioning is indicated also by the continuing controversy over religious instruction in the American public schools. The avowed central purpose of this instruction is to develop at an early age the belief that leads to acceptance of religious authority. Doubts about the desirability of such conditioning and the resulting exercise of power, combined with irreconcilable differences of view as to the religious authority to be accepted, led to the original constitutional barrier to all such instruction. Those who seek the resulting power have never accepted this ban. They continue to encourage the implicit conditioning that comes from even such modest religious observances as voluntary and silent prayer. These, in turn, are seen by those opposing them as a source of eventual religious belief with its associated submission to religious authority. Other controversies, that over sex education being a prominent example, reflect the importance that is attached to social conditioning by the schools and the resulting submission (or nonsubmission) to authority that follows (or is believed to follow) from the beliefs that are thereby instilled. The often venomous character of the dispute over religious or sex education can only be understood when it is fully appreciated that power is involved.

5

It is tempting to think of most conditioning with its counterpart submission and associated exercise of power as something that is won by overt methods, as through the educational system or the media. There is a strong tendency to attach primary importance to what can be seen or heard. However, all societies have a yet more comprehensive form of social conditioning. It is sufficiently subtle and pervasive that it is deemed a natural and integral part of life itself; there is no visible or specific effort that wins the requisite belief and submission. Thus parental authority need not in most cases be asserted; it is seemingly normal and what all children by nature accept. And similarly the authority of the schoolteacher and priest. And of community leaders. And of the nation's duly elected officials and those who collect taxes and enforce the laws. Partly because it is the communal tendency and instinct, one renders service to an employer and manifests the scripturally enjoined behavior of the good and faithful servant. Specific instruction is not generally thought necessary against murder, rape, or even theft. Such implicit conditioning bears comprehensively but subjectively and invisibly upon the individual from birth. We cannot assess its importance in relation to overt conditioning, but neither can we doubt that it is important.

34

6

Once belief is won, whether by explicit or implicit conditioning, the resulting subordination to the will of others is thought to be the product of the individual's own moral or social sense — his or her feeling as to what is right or good. In the pure case this is wholly separate from compensatory reward or condign punishment. Just as children obey parents, so adults bathe, use a deodorant, go to church, or surrender to the views of a political leader; it is the proper or personally rewarding thing to do; punishment or reward is not involved. However, in the common case the three instruments of enforcement are combined. Children yield to parental authority as a matter of course. But present also may be the promise of compensatory reward for submission and the possibility of condign punishment for resistance. As a similar result of family and social conditioning many individuals submit to religious authority; some, however, still contemplate the imaginatively unpleasant treatment that ultimately awaits those who fail to do so. It is sufficient for many adults that they should be good citizens and thus submit to their government. But there is also tangible compensation in the form of position, employment, and social esteem for the person who so yields. And for the individual who rejects the conditioned view of acceptable behavior the punishment by the community or more directly by authority can be severe. Never in the consideration of power can we assume that there is only one source or one instrument of power at work.

7

An important dividend from separating power into its anatomical components is that we see that what often are taken to be differences in kind are, in fact, differences in degree.[6] And the constituent elements are of different force in each instance. Thus the exercise of power by totalitarian regimes combines a peculiarly intensive (and preclusive) use of conditioned enforcement — by schools, press, television, radio, oratory — with large compensatory reward for those who conform and condign punishment, often of a permanent sort, for those who do not. In the 1930s and 1940s, the massive propaganda of Joseph Paul Goebbels in Germany was a much-remarked feature of National Socialism, a major resort to overt conditioned power. It was combined, however, with the powerful compensatory attraction of jobs and war contracts. And there was the condign punishment of the concentration camps for those who still resisted subordination. Similarly in Stalinist Russia; there, too, compensatory reward, condign punishment, and overt conditioning were all fully deployed. In other cases the admixture was or is more selective. The Latin American dictators Rafael Trujillo and Anastasio Somoza had special reputations for cruelty because, having little skill in the exercise of conditioned power (with little plausible beneficence to proclaim) and few resources to call on for compensatory power, they were forced to rely nearly totally on condign power. This has led to a distinction between authoritarian power, with its more or less exclusive reliance on condign enforcement, and the more comprehensive use of condign, com-

[6] Although differences in degree, we should always be reminded, can be remarkably different.

pensatory, and conditioned power that is characterized as totalitarian power. South American, African, or Asian dictators are authoritarian; the Communist countries are totalitarian. And it has been further held[7] that the authoritarian exercise of power, being limited, is morally superior to the more comprehensive totalitarian exercise. This is not a distinction of particular merit for those subject to the authoritarian regimes. The latter's greater need to rely on condign power and associated cruelty and death can easily be the more uncomfortable or offensive of the two.

Democratic governments do not eschew condign, compensatory, or conditioned power; all these are exercised. The difference again is in the combination involved, the constraints to which the instruments are subject, and, an important point, the extent to which the state reserves to itself the exclusive use of conditioned power.

Always in considering the exercise of power, we must be sensitive to the differing combinations of the component parts. These varied combinations and their permutations will extensively concern us in the pages to come. And we shall see the reality that is largely concealed in references to economic, political, religious, and other power. None of them can be understood, however, except as we see the elements of which they are composed, so first we must look at the sources of power.

[7] Notably by the administration of President Reagan and particularly by his Ambassador to the United Nations, Mrs. Jeane Kirkpatrick.

IV

The Sources of Power
Personality

The Prime Minister out of office is seen, too often, to have been but a pompous rhetorician, and the General without an army is but the tame hero of a market town.
— W. SOMERSET MAUGHAM
The Moon and Sixpence

WE COME NOW to what lies behind the instruments for the enforcement of power adumbrated in the last chapters, what allows of the exercise of condign, compensatory, and conditioned power in their various forms and mixtures.

Three things provide such access: personality, property, and organization. As in the case of the instruments of enforcement, these, the ultimate sources of power, appear nearly always in combination. Personality is much enhanced by property and vice versa; it usually has the added strength that comes from organization. Property always exists in association with organization and, not infrequently, with a dominant personality. Organization, in turn, is augmented and supported by both property and personality.

Each of the three sources of power has a strong, though never exclusive, relationship with a specific instrument of enforcement. Organization is associated with conditioned power; property, needless to say, with compensatory power.

38

Personality has an original and long-standing association with condign power; anciently individuals achieved submission by superior physical prowess, which is to say the ability to inflict punishment of a physical nature on the recalcitrant or nonconformist. This traditional association still has a certain resonance in the modern world. It remains particularly important among children; there is a natural deference in any group of youngsters to the physically strongest boy or, on occasion, girl. One who makes unduly promiscuous or conspicuous use of this source of condign enforcement is celebrated and condemned as a bully. It is taken for granted that as children mature and become presumptively more civilized, they will resort to such condign power less and less and its source in personality will recede in importance.

The connection between the two will, however, continue to influence attitudes. Mythically or historically important leaders — Hercules, Peter the Great, Charles de Gaulle — are assumed to have owed some of their power to their physical strength or size. They are spoken of as *commanding* figures. Napoleon was remarkable partly because he was so small. There remains in all modern societies a tendency to defer, that is, in a minor way to submit, to the tall or otherwise physically impressive figure. A bias in favor of tall men, and against very short ones, is still one of the few acceptable forms of discrimination in the modern community. One speaks of a disagreeable, offensive, or nasty *little* man, adding the final adjective as the ultimate insult; no equally adverse connotation is attached to *big*.

However, it is a commonplace that those most celebrated in history for their personal power — Moses, Confucius, Aristotle, Plato, Jesus, the Prophet, Marx, Gandhi — owed little or nothing to their physical strength or their personal resort to condign power. Less evident qualities accorded them the ability to bend millions or hundreds of millions durably to their will. Soon, of course, more than just personality was required; associated lawgivers, temples, schools, apostles, churches, mosques, the First International, or the Congress party were brought to their support. Organization and a not insignificant amount of property thus came to sustain and enhance the originating personality as sources of power. But none can doubt the initial importance of personality in winning belief, and it was this belief — conditioned power — that gave strength, impetus, and credence in all of these instances.

2

In the modern community the most important association of personality has now become this connection with conditioned power. The effective personality wins submission by persuasion — by cultivating belief, by "exercising leadership." Which specific aspects of personality give access to conditioned power are among the most discussed questions of our time and, indeed, of all time.[1] Of great past and some present importance is the conviction of the individual effectively conveyed to others that he or she is in communication with a supernatural force and guidance not available to people at large. Thus the following of countless religious leaders, as also of Joan of Arc, Philip II, and General Douglas MacArthur. At a more commonplace level, mental resource, precision, and acuity, charm, seeming honesty, humor, solemnity, and much more can be important. So also the ability to express thought in cogent, eloquent, repetitive, or otherwise compelling terms.

[1] See, for example, Max Weber and his concept of charismatic leadership. Reinhard Bendix, *Max Weber: An Intellectual Portrait* (Garden City, N.Y.: Doubleday, 1960), pp. 301 et seq.

There are other personal qualities giving access to conditioned power that have no close relationship either to intelligence or expression. A supreme certainty in the individual's own belief and assertion is of prime importance for winning belief and submission in others, and this personal trait is not necessarily related to intelligence. It can, indeed, be the reverse. It is a basic characteristic of economic, foreign, and military policy, and much business policy, that the connection between any particular action and its result is uncertain at best and quite frequently unknown. No one can say for sure what the ultimate consequence of a particular increase in interest rates, a proposed gesture of political support to some recidivist government, an elaborately planned military or war initiative, will be. Or what the return will be from some business endeavor. Power in these cases — submission to will — regularly passes to those who are able to assert the unknown with the greatest conviction. Power accrues not to the individual who knows; it goes to the one who, often out of obtuseness, believes that he knows and who can persuade others to that belief.

3

An important tendency in all modern political comment is to exaggerate the role of personality in the exercise of power. A great number of factors coalesce to cause this error; the first is the historical eminence of the great leader. Many such figures, from Moses to Marx, to Hitler, to Stalin, to Winston Churchill and Franklin D. Roosevelt, had an unquestioned ability to convert or subdue others to their purposes. Their personalities gave them varied access to condign, compensatory, and conditioned power. Such men and, as a form of echo, many far more commonplace figures in high position are much celebrated and admired. What rightly should be attributed to the property or organization surrounding them is thus accorded to their personality.

Vanity also contributes to the exaggeration of the role of personality. Nothing so rejoices the corporate executive, television anchorman, or politician as to believe that he is uniquely endowed with the qualities of leadership that derive from intelligence, charm, or sustained rhetorical capacity — that he has a personal right to command. And when he believes it, so do others.

What may be called the sycophantic effect is another cause of the enhancement of personality as a source of power. The individual who has access to the instruments of power has a natural attraction for those who wish to share his influence, live in his shadow. It would not be seemly to tell him his access to power came from his money; it does not serve the purposes of flattery to say it really belongs to the organization of which he is a part. So it is said — and he is told — that it is his personality, his qualities as a leader, that accord him his power. This, again, both he and others come to believe.

Then there is the modern phenomenon of the synthetic, or created, personality, something of no slight importance. Personality, as noted, reflects an earlier and more primitive stage in the exercise of power; thus it appeals to the archaic instinct that controls much of the comment on these matters. It is also more interesting than organization. And far more readily than organization, it appeals to the reporters, television commentators, and others who deal with the exercise of power and who associate it with what speaks, walks, and is seen. As a highly practical matter, people can give interviews and appear on television; organizations cannot.

The consequence is that personality traits are attributed to heads of organizations that seem appropriate to the power exercised, and this imagery is assiduously and professionally cultivated. It is the principal purpose of much public relations effort. Cabinet members, other public officials, and presidents of corporations are examples of the extensively synthesized personality; journalists and commentators of the more vulnerable sort are persuaded of their unique personal qualities, as are the subjects themselves. There is proof of this phenomenon in what happens to a head of General Motors or a secretary of defense on the day he retires or leaves office. Divorced from organization, the synthetic personality dissolves, and the individual behind it disappears into the innocuous obscurity for which his real personality intended him.[2]

It is the nature of common social observances to dramatize the role of personality as well. In the modern capital, Washington being no doubt the extreme case, a very large part of all social and other intercourse is concerned with who is exercising power — who is imposing his or her purposes on others. And most social effort consists in seeking association with those who are deemed to be powerful. This attention is much cherished by those who receive it, and, in consequence, politicians, public officials, journalists, and others cultivate a public aspect that suggests power. In dress, manner, and general behavior they present a well-

[2] While a greater appreciation of the synthetic personality would add substantially to our understanding of the sources of power, its existence is already in no slight measure perceived. A specific reference to the synthetic personality is not unknown. Or to the plastic personality, which has the same connotation. The frequent statement that the head of a corporation or government agency is "really just an organization man" recognizes that the individual's personality is a derivative of the group to which he belongs.

studied appearance of leadership and command. Their conversation turns frequently and often ostentatiously on how the speaker's will is being imposed on others. The result is often quite convincing.

4

The rituals of politics — meetings, audiences, and applause — lead also to a misapprehension of personality as a source of power. This is what may be called the histrionic effect. The political orator speaks regularly to audiences that are already fully conditioned in their belief. And he adjusts his thought and expression, often automatically, to what he knows to be that belief. The ensuing applause is then taken to be a measure of *his* influence, *his* power. His formidable personal traits — his personality — are believed to be the source of this power. In truth, he is showing only his aptitude for identifying with the conditioned belief of his constituency. His power is that of the preacher who, correctly judging the rain clouds, proceeds to pray for rain.

Many instances of this error could be cited. One of the most interesting examples from the American scene was William Jennings Bryan, considered by many the most influential orator of his age; his huge and responsive audiences were thought to be bent strongly to his will. His talent, which was far from negligible, consisted in attracting the already-conditioned to his meetings and in telling them what they wanted to hear. The applause and the amens came not from the newly persuaded but from those who were confirmed by him in their own earlier instinct or belief.

The word *leader*, as commonly used, is ambiguous and should be so regarded. The leader may be accomplished in

44

gaining the submission of others to his purposes. But in the everyday reference he is as often merely adept at identifying himself with the conditioned will of the crowd and identifying for the crowd its own purposes.

5

The relationship of the compulsive orator to his applauding audience, the political candidate to his approving voters, the evangelist to his receptive throng, is not, then, a pure exercise of power. As often, it is a submission by the presumed leader to the will — the conditioned beliefs — of his constituency. This also is recognized; here, as elsewhere, there is a popular sense of the deeper truth. The politician whose principal skill is in identifying himself with the people as distinct from the one who has the ability to persuade and command is considered a demagogue. His performance is described as "playing to the crowd." These derogatory references correctly analyze his relationship to power: his personality has the appearance but not the reality of a source of power.

Nevertheless, the individual who accommodates his views to the beliefs and aspirations of the crowd cannot be wholly dismissed. Nor can personality as a source of power. Involved in the common case is a contract. A would-be leader possessing the requisite personal traits and qualities recognizes the will of the relevant constituency and identifies himself with it. But because he does so, his constituency agrees, on some matters, to accept *his* will. He tells his followers, as they are called, what their own conditioning has told them they should believe or it is in their interest to believe. They, in turn, accept his expression of their belief and follow him on variations, notably on the means for giving it practical effect. A person of true power is one who, as part of this bargain, is able to win acceptance for substantial views of his own. A person of slight power conforms fully and exclusively to the beliefs of the crowd. Martin Luther King, Jr., knew and voiced what his constituency wanted, but he guided it extensively on the action that realized those aims. So did Franklin D. Roosevelt. And others. How truly powerful a leader is can be judged by how well he can persuade his followers to accept his solutions to their problems, his path to their goals.

6

Inevitably, as personality comes into close association with its constituency, a structure develops. The politician comes to have what is called an organization or, if the structure seems notably firm, a machine. The effective labor leader achieves a strong union, the capable businessman a well-managed enterprise, the religious leader a church and congregation. Personality uniformly seeks the reinforcement of organization.

It also enhances its power by buying submission, a thing not unknown to the politician, historically important in the role of religious leadership, and central to the power of the business executive. Accordingly, we will now consider the role of property, the source of that payment. Thereafter we will come to organization, the third and, in the modern world, the transcendent source of power.

V

The Sources of Power
Property

I would say exploitation was the crunch issue . . . For exploitation read *property* and you have the whole bit. First the exploiter hits the wage-slave over the head with his superior wealth; then he brainwashes him into believing that the pursuit of property is a valid motive for breaking him at the grindstone. That way he has him hooked twice over.

— JOHN LE CARRÉ,
The Little Drummer Girl

OF THE THREE sources of power, property is seemingly the most forthright. Its possession gives access to the most commonplace exercise of power, which is the bending of the will of one person to another by straightforward purchase. The employer thus bends workers to his purpose, the man of wealth his chauffeur, the special-interest group its kept politicians, the lecher his mistress. The association between property and compensatory power is so simple and direct that in the past it has been considered comprehensive. For socialists property was and in some measure remains not only the decisive but the sole source of power, the integument that held and holds the capitalist system together. As long as it remains in private hands, no others can possess power. "The theory of the Communists may be summed up in the single phrase: Abolition of private property."[1] Adolf Berle, who over a long life concerned himself more deeply than any other American writer with the nature of power, dwelt at length and with perception on the way in which in the modern large corporation the management rather than the owners of the property, that is, the shareholders, emerges as the decisive holder of power. This he rightly considered to be in sharp contrast with accepted belief. One of his several books on the subject he called *Power Without Property*.[2] Any search for the improper use of power turns automatically to the misuse of money, which is to say property — to the bribery of legislators or public officials or by contractors or of foreign governments.

Especially on the left in politics, but to some extent on the right, it is still a manifestation of a direct and muscular intelligence to concede and emphasize the decisive power that accrues to property. What else in unvarnished judgment can be so important? And on occasion nothing is. In the United States in 1980, a congressman arrested in the so-called Abscam raids for accepting a bribe was heard to summarize a common view of compensatory reward derived from property as opposed to persuasion derived from personality or social conditioning: "Money talks," he said, "but bullshit walks."

In fact, as we have seen, property is but one of three sources of power, and in recent times its importance has been declining in relation to organization. The power in the business firm and the state that once emanated from property — from financial resources — now comes from the structured association of individuals, from bureaucracy. The access of property to the instruments of power has also

[1] Karl Marx and Friedrich Engels, *The Communist Manifesto*.
[2] Subtitling it *A New Development in American Political Economy.* (New York: Harcourt, Brace, 1959.)

48

been diminishing. Once it had condign power for winning submission; privately owned property accorded the right to punish slaves, servants, or serfs and allowed of resort to public authority to subdue worker dissent. This is no longer approved or sanctioned. In political life the direct purchase of submission is also in decline. Its modern importance in public affairs, which is not negligible, derives from the access pecuniary resources give to persuasion — to conditioned power. The modern man of wealth no longer uses his money to purchase votes; he contributes it to the purchase of television commercials and by this means hopes to win conditioned submission to his political will.

2

Property has, in truth, always accorded a measure of access to conditioned belief. In past times, notably in the latter years of the last century, so great was the prestige of property that, quite without the need for any actual compensation, it accorded power to its possessor. What the man of wealth said or believed attracted the belief of others as a matter of course. Such was the good fame of the rich, in Thorstein Veblen's phrase, that they had automatic access to both compensatory *and* conditioned power.

Thus the social thought of the elder John D. Rockefeller was not, in fact, more perceptive than that of a college sophomore of modest attainments. Coming as it did, however, from reputedly the richest man in the United States, it attracted major attention. In consequence, his views were influential on the benignity of wealth, on thrift, and on the improvement of the race by Social Darwinism and the social euthanasia of the poor (and therefore weak). So it was also with the elder J. P. Morgan. His case before a congressional committee that, in lending money, character is of more concern than assets was widely reported, long-remembered, and, it seems likely, somewhat believed. Legislators and others approved the purposes of Rockefeller and Morgan often without immediate thought of compensation. What the rich wanted, supported as it was by their property, was right.

There remains to this day the feeling on the part of men of means that their views on politics, economics, and personal behavior or decorum are meant, because of their wealth and associated precedence, to be taken seriously. Few people are so pained when they are ignored or made subject to the indecently asserted opinions of someone whose right to speech is not backed by the requisite assets.

However, wealth per se no longer gives automatic access to conditioned power. The rich man who now seeks such influence hires a public relations firm to win others to his beliefs.[3] Or he contributes to a politician or a political action committee that reflects his views. Or he goes into politics himself and uses his property not to purchase votes but to persuade voters. Social conditioning so purchased is the most visible current manifestation of the power deriving from property.

3

It was not so in the past. In the early industrial communities, the American company town being the classic case, submission to the purposes of the employer was purchased under circumstances where alternatives to such submission

[3] The elder Rockefeller eventually succumbed to this need and hired the pioneer publicist Ivy Lee to add explicit social conditioning to that implicitly associated with his property.

were either nonexistent or extremely unpleasant. Nor was compensatory power the only instrument of enforcement. In combination with the sanguinary personality of the owner, property gave access to condign power through the local government and the police. And through local newspapers, churches, and other public expression, it gave access to conditioned power as well.

Such power no longer derives from property. More civilized attitudes curbing the access to condign power receive some of the credit. As does the rise of the trade union.[4] The forthright payment of politicians came into conflict with the improving ethics of the age — the too-obviously-purchased congressman or governor declined in public esteem.

More important were the increase in affluence and its expression in the modern welfare state. Compensatory power at its greatest required that there be few or no sources of income other than that of the property owner; with affluence came widened employment opportunities. Income rising above the level of mere subsistence is also a liberating force. Work is no longer compelled, or so compelled, by stark need. And, as earlier noted, unemployment compensation, welfare benefits, medical care, and retirement funds lead, in similar fashion, to a loosening of the constraints of compensatory power and thus to a lessened importance of its source in property. It is one of the curiosities of much social comment that such welfare measures are regularly seen as limitations on freedom — the freedom presumptively inherent in the free enterprise system. Less mention is made of the escape they accord from the compensatory power once associated in compelling form with property.

But the decline in the power deriving from property, as

---

[4] The dialectic of power — its tendency to provoke an opposite and countervailing exercise of power — is discussed in chapters VIII and IX.

also in that deriving from personality, is, most of all, to be attributed to the rise of organization. This is true in the state; there both the power that comes from wealth and the power that comes from personality have extensively surrendered to that deriving from organization.[5] It is in keeping with the dialectic of power that this, in turn, has given rise to the resistance, antipathy, and anger embodied in the common references to governmental bureaucracy. And organization — the vast administrative apparatus — has also now replaced property (and personality) as the ultimate locus of power in the modern large business enterprise.

The Rockefeller family is a metaphor of this change. Of the four Rockefeller grandsons who survived to the latter 1970s, two — John D., III, and Laurance — were noted principally for their wealth and philanthropy. Two — Nelson and David — were involved with massive public and private organizations — the State of New York, the government of the United States, and the Chase Manhattan Bank. The brothers whose association was with property were little known, personal acolytes and the professional New York philanthropoid community apart. The two who were associated with organization were widely heard and indubitably influential, that is, *powerful.* When he was under examination by the Congress for the post of Vice President, Nelson Rockefeller had to defend at some length his practice of using his wealth to reward and thus to ensure the loyalty, meaning submission to his purposes, of various political

---

[5] In 1917, Vladimir Ilyich Lenin came to the position of supreme authority in what had been Imperial Russia. Central to his assertion of power was the suppression of privately owned property as a source. By the time of his death seven years later, he had seen — and strongly stressed — the existence and further emergence of another source of power, that of the huge bureaucracy the socialist state required. Private property as a source of power had given way to organization as a source of power.

52

subordinates. In the last century such purchase of acolytes would have been thought routine in American politics, but by the time Rockefeller appeared before the congressional committee, it had become an abuse of power, albeit one of minor effect.

Nonetheless, a sense of perspective must be maintained. Property is not now all-important as a source of power, but that is far from saying that it is unimportant. Through compensatory power it wins the daily submission of the worklives of millions. And it helps win the effort, as well as the belief, of those who guide the great economic enterprises. Its obvious connection with the purchase of conditioned power has already been stressed. In both the direct submission it purchases from civilians and soldiers and the massive support it wins from the weapons industry, it plays a large role in the most awe-inspiring of the modern manifestations of power, that of the military establishment. Let no one suppose that property, having yielded to organization as the principal source of power, is now in any measure to be ignored.

VI

The Sources of Power
Organization I

ORGANIZATION, the third of the sources of power, normally exists in association with property and, in greater or less measure, with personality. It is, however, more important than either, and in modern times increasingly so. "No collective category, no class, no group of any kind in and of itself wields power or can use it. Another factor must be present: that of organization."[1] Some scholars, among them Charles E. Lindblom, hold that organization, including that manifested in government, is the ultimate source of *all* power.[2] There is a case here; property and personality have effect only with the support of organization. However, they are in greatly varying combination with it, universal though organization may be. One understands the

[1] Adolf A. Berle, Jr., *Power* (New York: Harcourt, Brace and World, 1969), p. 63.

[2] "Some people believe that wealth or property is the underlying source of power. But property is itself a form of authority created by government." Charles E. Lindblom, *Politics and Markets: The World's Political-Economic Systems* (New York: Basic Books, 1977), p. 26.

54

effect of the combination of the sources of power only as one first sees the constituent elements.

2

The dictionary definition of organization — "a number of persons or groups . . . united for some purpose or work" — expresses its essential character. The participants, in one degree or another, have submitted to the purposes of organization in pursuit of some common purpose, which then normally involves the winning of the submission of people or groups external to the organization. However, the word, as used, covers a striking diversity in association and in the degree of relevant internal and external submission. Thus an army is an organization; it has a strong internal structure that accords each man his appropriate place and authority; it exacts a high level of obedience — of submission — from its members. And externally from those whom it impresses, frightens, or conquers and subdues.

An American political party is also an organization. Here internal structure is largely absent; so is any appreciable submission by its members to the purposes of the organization. The individual who adjusts his belief or expression to what he believes to be the will of the party may, indeed, be celebrated as a party loyalist, but equally he may be called a party hack. The external submission which the party wins as an organization is erratic and often slight.

A corporation is an organization. It exacts a high level of internal submission but, as compared with a political party, over a narrower range of matters — in the main, though by no means exclusively, activities concerned with the production and sale of goods and services. It seeks external submission in the form of purchase and use of those goods and services by its customers. And it seeks submission to its purposes by the state.

Government is an organization. It enforces internal submission on its members in a highly diverse fashion for greatly diverse external purposes. On military matters the internal submission of members of the organization is comprehensive; indiscipline is not countenanced. As just noted, external submission when sought — when military force is applied — is likewise comprehensive. In other areas of government the internal submission to the purposes of the organization is much less; a certain amiable self-expression is assumed. And the external submission — obedience to traffic laws, laws against shoplifting or the littering of streets — is relatively slight.

So diverse are the participants, the purposes, and the degree of submission covered by the word *organization* that one's first reaction is to wonder what sense can be made of the subject. In fact, the idea of organization yields to surprisingly comprehensive and consistent rules. Organization can have access to condign power; in its normal association with property it has access to compensatory power; overwhelmingly, and especially in its modern form, organization has access to conditioned power. In fact, it is for the exercise of conditioned power that most organization is brought into existence.

There are three further characteristics of organization as a source of power. The first is its bimodal symmetry: it wins submission to its purposes outside the organization only as it wins submission within. The strength and reliability of its external power depend on the depth and certainty of the internal submission.

The power of an organization is dependent also, not surprisingly, on its association with the other sources of power — a point to which I will return — and on its access

56

to the instruments of enforcement. An organization is strong when it has effective access to all three of the latter — condign punishment, compensation, and conditioning — and weak as that access is less effective or missing.

Finally, there is an association between the power of an organization and the number and diversity of the purposes for which submission is sought. With the notable exception of the state, the more diverse the purposes on which an organization seeks to enforce its power, the weaker it will be in gaining submission to any one of them.

To these clarifying principles and their application, I now turn in this and the following chapter.

3

The bimodal symmetry of organization is its most obvious, most important, and, curiously enough, one of its most frequently overlooked features. As noted, the individual submits to the common purposes of the organization, and from this internal exercise of power comes the ability of the organization to impose its will externally. On the one depends the other. This is the invariable feature of all exercise of organized power.

The trade union illustrates the point. Its members, whatever their individual preferences or personal plans, accept its goals regarding wages, working conditions, and other benefits. And regardless of their needs or desires, they forgo work and pay in the event of a strike. On this internal submission depends the external power of the union — its ability to win the submission of the employer or, on occasion, the government. If union solidarity, the synonym for effective internal discipline or submission, is high, then the chance of winning union demands or of successful strike action is good. Power is effectively exercised. If scabs, stooges, stoolies, or men of otherwise reluctant or recalcitrant tendency abound in the ranks, the chance of success is less. Thus does external power derive from internal power. The unflattering terms by which the recalcitrants are characterized suggest the importance that is attached to internal discipline.

As with the union, so with all organization. A sternly disciplined army — one with strong internal submission — has external power and is effective against its enemy. One without such discipline has and is not. In the eighteenth and nineteenth centuries the minuscule British army and the British-led Indian army won victory after victory as the British moved north and west from Madras and Calcutta, invariably against forces greatly superior in infantry numbers and sometimes superior in artillery as well. Though there were setbacks, there was never a final defeat. The British forces had a strong internal organization from which came their external power. The submission of the individual soldier to the purposes of the army extended to a full acceptance of the idea of death, were it required. The soldiers of the opposing Indian princes made no similar submission and took a far more thoughtful view of personal danger. Internal power being less rigorously exercised, external power was appropriately less.

There are many other examples. The modern corporation depends for its effectiveness in producing and selling its product — that is, its ability to win external submission — on the quality of its internal organization, which is to say the extent and depth of the submission of its employees. This is not comprehensively urgent in the bottom ranks of the enterprise; there a sufficient submission can be had by the routine exercise of compensatory power. (Some point may, indeed, be made as well of the importance of high morale, that is, conditioned power, in the work force; in recent times this, for example, has been much emphasized in explaining Japanese industrial success.) The position changes markedly as one proceeds to the upper executive ranks. There full subordination to the purposes of the firm is essential. Expression or action in conflict with corporate purpose is unthinkable. No senior executive would presume to suggest that the cigarettes his company manufactures cause cancer, that its automobiles are unsafe, that its pharmaceuticals are medically suspect. Or that some political initiative sought by the company — improvement of depreciation allowances or the reduction of foreign competition — is in conflict with the public interest. It is on such internal discipline, no less than with the British army in India, that external power depends. High salaries are collected for such submission, but it would be wrong to suggest that these are the decisive factor. Belief in the purposes of the corporation — conditioned power — is almost certainly more important.

Because this is conditioned power, it follows that it does not hurt, is often not even noticed by, the individual subject to it. There are few people who so willingly and completely submit to the power of the organization with so little consciousness of submission as the modern corporate executive. Not being a conscious act, it is not derogatory or painful. Like the submission of Tolstoy's soldier to the rule of the regiment, it can be a welcome relief from the rigors of personal thought and decision. The corporate belief and need are there to be accepted.[3]

[3] Although this is not entirely without conflict for those involved. On this, see the revealing chapter "The Executive Ego" in William H. Whyte, Jr.'s classic study *The Organization Man* (New York: Simon and Schuster, 1956), pp. 150–56. Whyte quotes an executive as saying, "A help-wanted ad we ran recently asked for engineers who would 'conform to our work patterns.' Someone slipped up on that

4

The relation between the internal and external expressions of power within organization can be seen in the public bureaucracy, professional associations, organized sport, and organized crime. Nothing so weakens the external power of a public agency — in the United States the Pentagon or the Department of State, for example — as the undisciplined expression of dissenting views from within. Thus the constant struggle to suppress such dissent. Nothing so undermines the power of physicians over their patients as the intemperate criticism of the competence of one doctor by another. Thus the professional code that avoids such criticism. Again we see the internal rules of conduct that protect the external exercise of power. Teamwork, a fully conditioned submission to the power of the organization, is the essence of success in organized sport.[4] And the case is the

---

one. He actually came out and said what's really wanted in our organization." Another executive put it more succinctly: "'The further up you go, the less you can afford to stick out in any one place.'" Whyte, p. 155.

[4] An interesting and also revealing metaphor on the sources and instruments of power is the athletic team — the American professional football team, for example. It is implicit in the discussion of the sport that all sources *and* instruments of power are there deployed, and it is accepted that success depends on the effectiveness of their use. The sources are personality (those of the coaches and the more spectacular or effective players); property (it takes the resources of more than a village to support a major team); and, most of all, the highly sophisticated organization comprising the players and coaches. The instruments of enforcement are the threat of condign rebuke from teammates, coach, and community; the pay or compensatory power, a matter on which players are far from negligent; and, above all, the highly developed training or conditioning manifest in the team's will to win. The team most strongly combining all of these elements of power will win; it will gain the submission of the opposing team. As in sport, so in life.

same with organized crime. No criminal gang can tolerate the open or covert cooperation with the police of any of its members. Predictably, any such failure in internal discipline — in acceptance of the purposes of the organization — invites a strong, usually lethal, condign response. When perceived, the principles governing organized power are seen to be pervasive.

And the same principles govern the exercise of political power. The external power of an American political party, its ability to win submission beyond its ranks, is negligible because internal discipline or submission is nonexistent. The principle extends further to the exercise of power by governments. In the last century and continuing to the first half of the present one, the Prussian-become-the-German state had formidable external power. That was because the Prussian idea required a comprehensive internal submission by the individual to the purposes of the state, including to its military enterprises. The external power of the United States in World War II — its ability to impose its purposes on its allies and the Germans and Japanese — was the counterpart of a strong internal submission to national purpose. There was far less such power against an infinitely weaker enemy in Vietnam because there was in that conflict — one may say fortunately — no similar submission. Internal power could not be developed in the context of what was widely perceived to be an unwise or feckless exercise of external power, and vice versa.

5

As compensatory reward has a natural association with property as a source of power, so social conditioning has a primary association with organization. The association is so taken for granted that it provokes little mention or even recognition. An individual or group seeking power organizes and then resorts automatically to persuasion. First a meeting is called, the unstated purpose of which is to consolidate belief within the organization — to get a maximum unity of internal power. This accomplished, an external advertising or educational program is launched.

The symmetry in organization between internal and external exercises of power extends to the instruments of enforcement. When external power relies principally on conditioning, so does internal power. And vice versa. The case is the same for condign and compensatory power; when these are used externally, they will be used internally. And again vice versa.

In dealing with conditioned power, it is taken for granted that members of a political, religious, or other group must be strongly and uniformly persuaded of its purposes if they are to be effective propagandists for those purposes externally. That, again, is why the history of the highly organized expressions of power — those of the Church, the Communist party, even the city political machine — is so extensively a chronicle of efforts to stamp out heresy. The nonsubmitting outsider may be reviled, but in the frequent case he arouses less antipathy and anger and invites less variously persuasive attention than does the dissident within.

It follows that strong organizations require the careful internal conditioning of their members for maximum external effect. The new recruit of the armed services or the Central Intelligence Agency is deeply and carefully drilled on the purposes of his organization. This is called indoctrination, a term that attests openly to the purpose of winning belief. Only when this belief is assured is the individual deemed qualified to pursue the external purposes of the organization. In the most commonplace of references, it is said that the *effective* or *good* official or officer is the one who believes in what he is doing — believes in his organization or outfit. The discomforting treatment of the dissident who breaks with the conditioned view — the Pentagon whistle blower, the unduly independent State Department officer, the recidivist of the CIA — affirms the point.

In its normal association with property, organization has access to compensatory as well as, on occasion, condign power. The business enterprise wins a good part of its external power by compensatory means — by offering the public something that is worth the surrender of money. That money, in turn, buys the effort and increases the compensatory power over those who serve the enterprise. It also advertises and merchandises the organization's products. That is to say, the organization also uses conditioned power; it cultivates belief in the merits of its products or services apart from their price — apart from the compensatory advantage in their purchase. It is considered an excellent thing that those engaged in advertising and selling a product believe in it themselves. Again the symmetry, although it is not universal; it is commonly said with some surprise that an individual "believes his own advertising."

The symmetry extends finally to condign power. As earlier noted, a military force imposes its will on the enemy by condign means, by the threat or reality of punishment of a notably sanguinary and painful sort. It wins internal submission by conditioning — by implanting belief in the purposes of the armed force and in the necessity for its members' absolute obedience to command. And this conditioning is supplemented by pay — by compensatory power. But symmetrically with the external exercise of condign power also goes a variety of compelling condign punishments in the event of soldierly default. All military organization accepts this need. All courts-martial or their equivalent have access to condign punishments that are harsher than those allowed by ordinary civilian processes. Thus the willingness of the soldier in combat to accept risk in inflicting condign punishment on his enemy is reinforced by the knowledge that he himself will be subject to similar punishment of greater or less severity if he fails to do so.

The symmetry between internal and external power is visible in other cases. The union that resorted to violence on the picket line against a recalcitrant employer in past times was likely to use the reality or threat of the same against insufficiently committed or backsliding members. The Mafia and other criminal organizations gain external power by the threat or reality of condign power. And this is also used internally to ensure the submission of their own members. In dealing with power, there are few absolutes. But the symmetry between internal and external means for the enforcement of power is sufficiently evident that it can be expected and even assumed.

VII

The Sources of Power
Organization II

THE BIMODAL SYMMETRY between its internal and external power is the first of the circumstances that bear on the ability of an organization to win submission to its purposes; I turn now to the other two. These are, as I've earlier indicated, first, the extent of its association with the two other sources of power and of its access to the three instruments of enforcement and, second, the diversity or concentration of its purposes.

An organization that has access to property and to personality in the form of leadership obviously gains power from this association. And if it has liberal access to the full range of condign and compensatory as well as conditioned power, this adds further to its strength. The clearest example of such a combination of the sources of power and instruments of enforcement is the totalitarian government. There all instruments and sources are brought to bear both internally in the government and externally and symmetrically on the public at large.

Internally, in the apparatus of the government of National Socialist Germany were the personality of Hitler, the financial, that is, property, resources of the Third Reich, and the highly effective bureaucracy with its roots in the traditions of the Prussian state. Proceeding from these sources of power was the condign punishment meted out to internal dissidents such as Ernst Roehm, who threatened Hitler's control of the party in the early days of Nazi rule, and those involved in the officers' revolt of July 20, 1944. There were also the compensatory power that sustained the bureaucracy, the S.S., and the Wehrmacht; the implicit conditioning from the tradition of disciplined service to the state; and the explicit conditioning of the propaganda of Hitler, Goebbels, and the party. Such was the internal power of the National Socialist government.

Externally, enforcing the submission of the populace as a whole, the instruments of power were the same. There were the condign action made evident by the concentration camps and the compensatory power flowing from public works — the *Autobahnen* — and later the vast government contracts available to arms manufacturers. And there was the implicit conditioning arising from the habit of obedience to the state reinforced by the explicit conditioning of the propaganda in combination with the monopoly or near-monopoly of access to the public mind, that is, to conditioned power. There has long been a tendency to associate power such as that exercised in Nazi Germany with a single source or a single instrument of enforcement — in the German case with the personality of Hitler or with the fear of the S.S. or with the peculiar persuasiveness of the concentration camps or with the propaganda of Goebbels. One sees how important it is to consider the whole diverse structure on which such power rests.

The response to Hitler by the governments of the United States and Britain in World War II invoked, it may be noted, the same sources of power and the same instruments of enforcement as were used by the Germans. The myth is of a total contrast; the fact is of different admixtures in different strengths. The personalities of Roosevelt and Churchill were of well-recognized importance. Economic resources — property — from highly developed industrial systems were a vital source of power, especially so in the case of the United States. And there was massive organization in both Allied countries. Proceeding from the same sources of power were the same instruments of its enforcement. Condign punishment was available for the few who gave ostentatious support to the enemy. There were jobs and other compensatory rewards. The force of social conditioning — patriotism — was very great.

The difference, to repeat, was in the strength of the instruments and in their admixture — both internally and externally. Condign punishment was of small importance for winning submission in the United States and Britain; so, on the whole, was explicit conditioning or propaganda, although it was not ignored. Compensatory power was, of course, important. But the yet more powerful instrument was implicit conditioning, the willing and more or less automatic acceptance of the national purpose. On this the common and self-congratulatory statement expressed a certain truth: the forces of freedom were, indeed, stronger than those of dictatorship. This was to say that the implicit conditioning leading to the self-motivated acceptance of the public purpose was more effective than the explicit conditioning won by overt propaganda or the threat of condign punishment on which, in much greater measure, the Nazis relied.

Since it has association with both property and personality and access to all the instruments of enforcement, a government is an especially strong organization, one of exceptional power. For this reason its power is inevitably viewed with awe and frequently with fear, and in all civilized societies it is agreed that there should be limits on the exercise thereof. Especially it is thought that there should be limits on the government's use of condign power. But there is also a strong feeling, openly expressed, against the undue use of explicit conditioning in the form of propaganda. There can even be criticism of implicit conditioning as a source of public power; as earlier noted, the politician who appeals too blatantly to patriotic or other conditioned belief is dismissed as a demagogue.

2

As with government, so with all other organization. Its ability to gain submission depends on the other sources of power — personality and property — with which it is associated, and on the instruments of power — implicit and explicit conditioning, compensatory and condign power — that it deploys. However, the third and final factor influencing the power of organization enters here: the number and diversity of its purposes. If the purposes of an organization are many and varied, both the sources and instruments of enforcement will have to be greater for a given effect than if the purposes are few and specific. An American political party, as already noted, is an organization of slight power. This is not only because of the limited sources of power on which it depends or the limited instruments it deploys. It lacks power, that is, the ability to win submission, because of the multitude of purposes it pursues. To have external power it must have internal agreement on the issues of economic policy, foreign policy, military policy, civil rights, welfare policy, health, education, social issues, and a host of other matters. Such agreement being impossible, it has no external expression or effect of any consequence.

In contrast with the weak political parties of modern times are the strong single-issue interest groups — the organizations opposing (or supporting) abortion, women's rights, gun control, and school busing and those favoring (or seeking to prevent) religious exercises in schools. These are effective because their members can unite on the single issue as they could not on more numerous matters. Internal submission is thus strongly in the service of external power.[1]

None of this is to say that single-issue politics is uniquely powerful — a common error of the time. On an issue such as abortion, the need for prayers in public schools, or the desirability of readily available firearms, a constituency can be united firmly in its belief, and from this will proceed the external effect. But these issues are still small in the great range of public concerns. In consequence, beyond a certain point, the constituency cannot be enlarged, and the external effect thus has limits. Also the narrowness of the issue makes possible and effective a countering conditioning and belief, the subject of the next chapter.

3

In speaking of organization as a source of power, a warning is in order — one that has to do with the illusion of power, a matter of much importance.

[1] Those pursuing single-issue politics have effective organization as the principal source of their power. And organization is in association with property and, on frequent occasion, with effective personality. Phyllis Schlafly, the Reverend Jerry Falwell, the Reverend Oral Roberts, and others demonstrate the role of personality; the money they collect reflects the important role of property.

The primary association of organization, as we have seen, is with conditioned power, an instrument of enforcement highly subjective in character. The individual who submits through conditioned belief is not aware of his submission; proceeding as it does from belief, it seems normal and right. And there is no objective indication of that submission visible to the one exercising the conditioned power. Individuals may be believed to have submitted to persuasion when they would have submitted anyway. Or the act of persuasion may be mistaken for the result. It follows that people can imagine that they are exercising conditioned power when, in fact, they are not. Others can suppose it where it does not exist. This is an exceedingly common illusion in our time. A writer in the presence of action of which he disapproves writes a book in support of the purposes he seeks. Though he may not attract many readers, he is persuaded that he has exercised power. Similarly the politician who makes a speech. And the journalist who writes an editorial, a column, or a thoughtfully slanted dispatch. Somewhere out there, there has been submission. Vanity usefully and influentially reinforces this impression. Much of what is called political power is, in practice, the illusion of power. So also the power of the press, a matter for later discussion.

There is a definite association between personality and the illusion of power. Individuals are notably susceptible to belief in their own persuasive abilities. So, perhaps especially, is the synthetic personality already mentioned. But the scope for illusion is greatly enhanced when organization is the primary source of the power. Those seeking to exercise power can give themselves the impression of its exercise by calling a meeting, assembling a committee, forming an organization, attending the ensuing gatherings, and reading the resulting press releases and manifestos. The will to exert power, to win submission, is satisfied not by the result but by the form. In such cases the organization that is the source of power serves as a substitute for the exercise of the power itself.

For an understanding of conditioned power and of organization as its source, the difference between the reality of power and the illusion of power must be firmly in mind. As later we come to examine the reality of the power of the military as opposed to that of peace groups, of corporations as opposed to consumer alliances and civic organizations variously in pursuit of public reform, this will be a distinction of first importance.

4

Power, especially when its source is in organization, is not a simple, forthright thing. We see how much is concealed in the familiar reference to a strong or powerful organization. Nor are all the limits on organized power yet in view. For, as individuals and organizations seek to extend their power — to win the submission of others to their individual or collective will — so others seek to resist that submission. And as personality, property, and organization and the associated instruments of enforcement are brought to bear in extending power, so they are brought to bear in resisting submission. It is this resistance, not any internal limits on the sources of power or the instruments of its enforcement, that provides the primary restriction on the exercise of power.

VIII

The Dialectic of Power I

So FAR our concern has been with how power is exercised and extended, but we must also understand how it is resisted, for this resistance is as integral a part of the phenomenon of power as its exercise itself. Were it otherwise, power could be extended indefinitely; all would be subject to the will of those best equipped in its use.

In fact, modern society is in equilibrium, more or less, between those who exercise power and those who counter it. We come now to the nature of this equilibrium — the way power creates its own resistance and acts to limit its own effectiveness.

2

One's first thought on being confronted with an unwelcome exercise of power is not always, and perhaps not normally, to seek means to resist it. Rather, it is how to achieve its dissolution — to say that the exercise is improper, illegitimate, unconstitutional, oppressive, or evil and that it should be curbed or prevented. Government is too powerful; accordingly, it should somehow be made less big, less intrusive, less comprehensive — something should be done to reduce its power. Corporations are too powerful; accordingly, they should be split up by the antitrust laws. Trade unions are too powerful; accordingly, they should be abolished or made subject to the right-to-work laws that give the individual worker the freedom to belong or not as he chooses. Men dominate women; accordingly, they should be persuaded or required to stand down and treat women as equals.

This would seem to be the logical first response to power; one seeks to limit or prevent its exercise. However, it is not the response to which, in actual practice, people generally resort. Nor is it the response that those resisting submission find most practical. The usual and most effective response to an unwelcome exercise of power is to build a countering position of power. The response to an arbitrary exercise of the power to tax was an organization to dump the tea so taxed in the water; to the draft, an organization of draft resisters; to an invasion of civil liberties, an organization to protect those liberties; to male chauvinism or dominance, an organization to assert women's rights.

So it is on all matters, large and small. The answer to the power of the employer is the union. And the answer to the union, a right-to-work law. The answer to the unwelcome exercise of religious authority is a countering church or doctrine. If the seller is overcharging, the buyer comes together with other buyers to boycott or to bargain. If teachers are unduly liberal in their ideas on sex education, parents come together to affirm the values of adolescent innocence and chastity. As so often happens in the exercise of power, the resort to countervailing power[1] is automatic.

[1] This is a term and concept that I first used in a narrower economic context in *American Capitalism: The Concept of Countervail-*

This responding exercise of power is of two kinds, direct and indirect. Directly it seeks personality, property, and organization that, in turn, allow it access to condign, compensatory, or conditioned instruments of power. These instruments are then exercised in opposition to the original power. Or the responding power is exercised indirectly through resort to the power of the state. If a corporation or union has unwelcome power, government regulation to restrict its exercise is sought. Or, alternatively, regulations having been imposed against an industry, the corporations involved seek to bring about their relaxation. A very large part of all modern political activity consists in efforts to capture the power of the state in support of, or in resistance to, some exercise of power.

3

We may lay it down as a rule that almost any manifestation of power will induce an opposite, though not necessarily equal, manifestation of power. Any effort to bend people to the will of others will encounter in some form an effort to resist that submission. On the relative effectiveness of these opposing forces depend the extent and effectiveness of the exercise of the original power.

We may also, as otherwise in these matters, discern a substantial symmetry between the manner in which power is extended and that by which it is resisted. This symmetry extends to both the sources of power and the instruments

---

ing Power (Boston: Houghton Mifflin, 1952, 1956; M. E. Sharpe, 1980). The notion that economic power is normally countered by an opposing position of power is one to which, obviously, I still adhere, and, in the years since I first made the case, it has won, I believe, a measure of acceptance. However, in that book I took an unduly sanguine view of the resulting equilibrium.

of enforcement. The power originating in personality is ordinarily answered by a strong personality; that originating in property is met by property; that having its origins in organization is normally countered by organization. And similarly as to the instruments of enforcement. Condign punishment is met by condign punishment, compensatory reward by compensatory reward. If the instrument of enforcement is social conditioning, explicit or implicit, this will also be the principal design for resistance. There are, of course, exceptions; some spectacular exercises of power have come from stepping outside this symmetrical framework, as I shall presently note. But symmetry in the dialectic of power is the broad rule. The classic struggle between employer and employee, capital and labor, again illustrates the point.

When workers first sought to resist submission to the power of employers on wages and working conditions, personality and countering personality were central to the exercise of power and to its resistance. And in keeping with the role of personality went condign measures of enforcement, including resort to the power of the state. In the great strike against the Carnegie Homestead Works in western Pennsylvania in 1892, the strikers, led by Hugh O'Donnell, acted in response to the powerful personality of Henry Clay Frick. Condign action by the workers was met by a symmetrical response, first from a flotilla of Pinkerton strikebreakers attempting a river-borne landing at the plant and subsequently (when the strike was crushed) from some seven thousand troops dispatched by Governor Robert E. Pattison of Pennsylvania.[2]

The great labor conflicts of the 1930s in the United States centered similarly on personality. The independent steel

[2] Philip Taft, *Organized Labor in American History* (New York: Harper and Row, 1964), pp. 136–42.

barons Ernest Weir and Tom Girdler, men of formidable personality, were opposed by the equally strong personalities of the union leaders John L. Lewis and Philip Murray. In Detroit the first Henry Ford, supported by Harry Bennett, the head of Ford Service, a condign enforcement instrument employing a substantial representation of local goons, gangsters, and unaffiliated ruffians, as well as more prosaic talent, was countered by the Reuther brothers and the other determined pioneers of the United Automobile Workers. In predictable association with personality went condign action and condign response. On May 26, 1937, the famous battle of the overpass occurred; the National Labor Relations Board said of the principal Ford plant at the time: ". . . River Rouge . . . has taken on many aspects of a community in which martial law has been declared, and in which a huge military organization . . . has been superimposed upon the regular civil authorities."[3]

Eventually, however, organization (along with property) replaced personal leadership as the source of employer power. Therewith went a shift in the instruments of enforcement and therewith also a change in the answering power of the workers. In the 1930s it had been the company leaders, men of strong personality such as Ford, Weir, and Girdler, along with Sewell Avery of Montgomery Ward, who had led the open and violent fight against the unions. The organization men of General Motors and the United States Steel Corporation did not resort to a similar condign response. Property, of course, remained a source of power. But the organization instinct was for negotiation. And personal vanity (as well as personal ownership of the property) was less involved. There was more concern for public opinion. In time and symmetrically, the unions came

[3] Allan Nevins and Frank Ernest Hill, *Ford: Decline and Rebirth, 1933–1962* (New York: Scribner's, 1963), p. 150.

to respond with the same sources and instruments of power. With some important exceptions, personal leadership ceased to be a central factor; violence diminished or disappeared. At first, property, in the form of the strike fund, became an important source of union power, bringing with it the ability on the union side to extend and last out a strike. Then a solid organization became even more important, and from this came an answering skill in negotiation and an answering capacity to carry the unions' case to the public. A nameless vice president for labor relations now sat down to negotiate on the company side; an almost equally anonymous executive joined him for the union. The strike — the comparative test of property resources — became a symbol of failure. Overwhelmingly, the source of power on both sides was organization. And, as might be expected, the instrument for making this organized power effective was persuasion — persuasion by each side of the other and by both of the community at large. Conditioned power almost wholly replaced condign and compensatory power.

4

The symmetry between the sources of power and the countervailing response has a certain classic clarity in the field of labor relations. But it is also evident in many other areas. In World War II, as noted, the perverse, malign, but unquestionably powerful personality of Adolf Hitler was answered by those of Churchill, Roosevelt, Stalin, and de Gaulle — a natural, even inevitable, opposition of personality to personality. In fact, Churchill came to power in large measure because in 1940 it became imperative that Britain have a figure who could match the Fuehrer in strength. Thus, as well as for other reasons, the replacement of Neville Chamberlain, the aging organization man, by a prime minister of more forceful and forthright personality.[4]

In modern times there is the awful condign power implicit in nuclear weapons; and their development and deployment by one superpower is answered with similar action by the other, an ominous symmetry of which much more must later be said. The business enterprise seeks to extend its influence over consumers by its advertising — by conditioned power. Those at whom the advertising is directed — whose submission is thus sought — resort to organizations committed to discovering the truth about products or demanding truth in advertising. The corporation attempting a corporate takeover appeals to the compensatory interest of the stockholders involved. To resist this, the corporation under attack urges the greater reward from the status quo. Or it arranges countering offers from a more acceptable source. Advocates of a deposit on bottles to ensure their return to the dispenser organize and raise money to win support for their purpose. Those resisting that purpose organize and raise money to persuade the public of the resulting costs. The politician's organization begets an answering organization; his appeals for money are matched by those of his opponent; if he is personable, an opposing personality must be imagined or synthesized; his commercials bring answering commercials. Symmetry extends through both the sources and the instruments of power.

---

[4] Of the three sources of power deployed in World War II — personality, property, and organization — the personality of the opposing war leaders received by far the greatest share of attention. This does not mean that, as compared with property or organization, it was the most important to the outcome of the hostilities. It simply had the easiest access to popular attitudes. Property and especially organization were less visible, less dramatic, but certainly more important.

5

While symmetry in enforcing power and in answering it must generally be assumed, it is not inevitable. There have been striking examples in history of countering or counter-vailing power that have depended for their effectiveness on their asymmetry.

Such asymmetry will be noticed in the conflict between religious and secular power discussed in chapter X. The secular power in the early Christian era relied on personality and resorted readily to condign action in enforcement. The religious power it frequently confronted had its source not insignificantly in personality and property but over-whelmingly in organization. From this organization came the belief, the social conditioning, that was always an effective instrument for enforcing its will.

More recently, the most notable cases of asymmetry in the exercise of countervailing power were those of Mohandas K. (Mahatma) Gandhi in contending with British authority in India, and of his disciple Martin Luther King, Jr., in opposing racial discrimination in the United States. The power of the British in India derived from the carefully culti-vated personal images of the Viceroy and the King Emperor or Queen Empress, the similarly cultivated revenue (that is, property) resources of the Raj, and the superb organization of the Indian civil and military administration. The com-pensatory reward for those who were in power or who accepted the social conditioning that urged the benignity of British rule was not unimportant. But the instrument of prime importance was the threat or reality of condign en-forcement from the military and the police.

Against the foregoing elements of British rule Gandhi offered his powerful personality and a substantial organization, and from both of these came social conditioning on the right of the Indians to rule themselves. But he did not proceed, as would have been expected, to build an armed force in opposition to that of the British — to bring condign power to bear on condign power. Instead he resorted to non-violence — passive resistance[5] to the exercise of British rule, including at various times resistance to the collection of taxes or the functioning of the courts, refusal to obey police orders, and other specific acts of civil disobedience. This departure from the accepted design was a source of infinite wonder, so deeply is symmetry assumed. Nonetheless, the Raj would have dealt in a matter of hours with any army Gandhi might have assembled, while in dealing with this asymmetrical resistance, it was recurrently at a loss and, in the end, defeated. There was a general parallel in Martin Luther King, Jr.'s efforts in the American South. Had the participants in the famous Selma march fought the local police, they would have been easily overcome. In choosing, asymmetrically, to refuse all invitations to answering violence, they too used a far less obvious but more formidable tactic. "Nonviolent resistance paralyzed and confused the power structures against which it was directed."[6]

Nevertheless, symmetry in both the sources of power and the instruments of enforcement remains the rule. This is affirmed in a dozen aphorisms: one fights fire with fire; force begets force; those who live by the sword shall die by the sword. Mahatma Gandhi and Martin Luther King, Jr., owe some of their fame to their success; they owe even more to their break with the accepted and accustomed dialectic of power.

[5] More precisely Satyagraha, which he distinguished from mere passive resistance and defined as "force which is born of truth and love or nonviolence."

[6] Martin Luther King, Jr., *Why We Can't Wait* (New York: Harper and Row, 1964), p. 30.

IX

The Dialectic of Power II
The Regulation of Power

THE BASIC DIALECTIC of power, its opposing and generally symmetrical exercise, is a process that intimately involves the modern state. A group or individual seeks the support of the state in winning the submission of others or for resisting the exercise of power by others. This effort then extends to secondary and tertiary manifestations — attempts to have the state directly suppress unwelcome exercise of power or to have it resist such suppression. Thus, in the last century, to recur to the example in the preceding chapter, employers successfully sought the intervention of the state to suppress trade union organization, the organization that was the source of the workers' power. And in this century trade unions have successfully sought the suppression by the state of the instruments of power by which employers countered union organization — they have won protection against the promiscuous use of the condign power of the police, of compensatory power in the form of payments to strikebreakers, and of conditioned power in

81

various forms of on-the-job persuasion. Employers, in turn, have come together to win passage of right-to-work laws. These have as their purpose preventing the unions from (as it is seen) enforcing the undue submission of their members or of potential workers who have not yet been unionized.

The dialectic of power is not uncomplicated, nor is the process by which it is regulated and controlled. It must first be noted that the state intervenes in a very different way as between the three instruments of power even while it accords a similar but by no means identical protection to the sources of power.

Specifically, the regulatory hand of the modern democratic state rests heavily on the exercise of condign power, but much less so on the exercise of compensatory power. And generally, if subject to much dispute, it protects most of the exercise of conditioned power. Going back to the sources of power, the state is, on the whole, tolerant of personality, protective of property, and in somewhat qualified defense of organization. These tendencies, in turn, are controlling influences on the associated dialectic of power and on those who seek the support of the state for the exercise of power or its suppression. What is fitting and legitimate as regards the role of the state in these matters is the bread and butter of much if not most political and other public debate.

2

All civilized communities, without exception, regulate the exercise of condign power. In modern Western societies its use is confined by public opinion and public law to the government, with some residual use on wives and children. In turn, the use of condign power by the state is closely regulated; some forms — cruel and unusual punishments in American constitutional parlance — are prohibited, and the propriety and utility of the death penalty or of mandatory jail sentences for certain popularly odious crimes are subject to avid and much-enjoyed discussion. Punishments are duly spelled out in law so as to make them reasonably consonant with the submission being sought. Those specified for murder are appropriately more severe than those for shoplifting or violation of the motor vehicle laws. There is then the massive apparatus of the courts, with their responsibility for deciding guilt or innocence as well as the more precise penalty called for in the particular case.[1]

Because the state has a general monopoly over the exercise of condign power, those seeking its use on their own behalf — for the submission they seek — must appeal to the state; such appeals — for stronger (or sometimes less strong) condign action against abortion, sex crimes, drug use, street violence, and much else — constitute a considerable part of modern political agitation.

The precision and effectiveness of the regulation of the use of condign power are, perhaps, the clearest index of the level of civilization in a community, and they are extensively so regarded in practice. Anarchy, such as that in modern Uganda or in Lebanon in the early 1980s, is principally marked by the unrestrained exercise of condign power both inside and outside the formal structure of government. What are called ruthless dictatorships — those, for example, of Trujillo, Somoza, and Duvalier in Central America and the

---

[1] This is not, of course, the only function of the courts. They are also an original source of power as they decide constitutional and legislative intent, with, at times, no slight range of discretion. I have deliberately, although not without some regret, by-passed the role of the courts in the regulation of power. It is partly a question of qualification and partly that I have very little to say on the subject and less, alas, that is new.

Caribbean, Stalin in Russia, and Hitler in Germany — are largely celebrated and remembered for their conspicuous use of condign power.

3

Compensatory power is similarly subject to regulation by the state, but unlike condign power, its use is also greatly protected in law and custom. The submission to the purposes of others that is won by compensation is, of course, central to the functioning of capitalism; compensatory reward as an inducement to toil is less noticed but not much less important in socialist societies. Nonetheless, numerous forms of compensatory power are regarded with disapproval or are specifically outlawed. Ostentatious payments to voters for their votes; bribes to public officials to influence legislation; the use of money in procuring customers and contracts, normally called kickbacks; and many other expressions of compensatory power are prevented by law or banned by public opinion.

Here also there is sharp conflict over the line dividing the approved use of power from the disapproved; the dialectic of power is again involved with what the state allows or forbids. Thus in recent times American corporations have been subject to a general prohibition against bribing foreign government officials and others to buy their products, that is, to submit to their commercial purposes. This regulation of compensatory power has, in turn, been strongly opposed by those who find it an impairment of a needed means for meeting foreign competition. As another example, an exceptionally tenuous line divides the forthright payment of compensation to a legislator for his favorable vote, a payment deeply disapproved in law and social mores, and a similar payment into his campaign fund or for a lecture appearance to buy a similar submission. The question of whether the state should forbid these latter manifestations of compensatory power is ardently debated.

4

Conditioned power is remarkable not because it is regulated by law but because it is explicitly protected by law in the free countries of the world. As condign power is prohibited to the private citizen, his freedoms of speech and expression, the bases of conditioned power, are specifically guaranteed. This protection, however, is by no means complete and again is a matter of much controversy. Personal vilification or slander and appeals to sanguinary violence, which is to say the threat of condign enforcement, are not, either in principle or in practice, defended — and in the frequent case they are forbidden. What is deemed to be Communist or on occasion socialist propaganda is thought by many to be outside the protection of law; at various times, including during the so-called McCarthy era, there was strong agitation calling for the suppression of such exercise of conditioned power and some effective government action to that end. There continues to be discussion over which forms of conditioning should be protected and which should be considered beyond the pale and hence regulated or suppressed.

In the United States the First Amendment to the Constitution guarantees the free exercise of conditioned power. In principle, this protection is greatly cherished, but in practice, when it defends disapproved submission to unwelcome or hostile ideas, it is gravely deplored, and there are ingeniously contrived efforts at exception or evasion. Indeed, the constitutional guarantee of the right of free speech owes much to the accident of time. It was enacted before the use of conditioned power became commonplace and central to the exercise of power — at a time when such use was the privilege of a small minority in the polity. Were the First Amendment being considered today, there would be fervent debate, and it would be passed only after notable exceptions — subversive political propaganda, pornography, encouragement of homosexuality and abortion — were carefully excluded from its protection. Or such would be the effort.

5

Turning now to the sources of power, there is, in general, no attempt by the state or to persuade the state to restrict or regulate personality. Socialist and Communist countries have, in the past, deplored and condemned cults of personality; such was the response, after the fact, to Joseph Stalin and Mao Tse-tung. In democratic countries, personality is accepted even if, on occasion, regretted as a source of power. The personalities of Franklin D. Roosevelt, John L. Lewis, George Wallace, Martin Luther King, Jr., and the Kennedy brothers were regarded by substantial numbers of people as inimical. Condign action in the form of assassination has been a sadly frequent response. But the support of the state in the suppression of adverse personality is not part of any common or normal political effort.[2]

The case of property is more complex. Traditional socialist doctrine held it to be a primary and even all-

[2] Exceptions can, of course, be found. The jailing of Gandhi by the British Raj and the long-time effort in the United States to deport the Australian-born labor leader Harry Bridges are examples of a forthright attempt to counter or suppress personality as a source of power.

embracing source of power. Accordingly, it could not be allowed to private individuals in more than minor amounts; for safety it had to be kept in public hands — in the more or less exclusive possession of the state. This principle is still respected in the Communist world. In nonsocialist doctrine, by contrast, property is so important as a source of power that it cannot wisely be concentrated in the hands of the government.

Accordingly, private property enjoys the general protection of the state in the nonsocialist world — in the United States through the constitutional guarantee of due process of law. But there remains the question of how extensively the state should intervene to get a wider distribution of property (and associated income) and thus of the power emanating therefrom. This sustains, in turn, one of the major political debates in the nonsocialist world, that over the distribution of wealth. And it leads on to such practical questions as the vigor of the enforcement of the antitrust laws, the appropriate progressivity of income taxes, and the incidence and distributional effect of other taxation. Much political advocacy also traces, in one way or another, to the restraint or nonrestraint of property in its relationship to power.[3]

As property as a source of power is both protected and regulated by the state, so also is organization. The rights of free assembly and association are strongly defended in

[3] On occasion bringing a convergence between the conservative defense of property as a personal right and the liberal (or left) assertion of its importance as a source of power. Called some years ago before a deeply conservative committee of the Texas legislature to explain and defend his ideas, the late Robert Montgomery of the University of Texas, a brilliant scholar of seriously suspect views, was asked sternly if he believed in private property. He replied, "I do, sir, and I believe in it so strongly that I want everyone in Texas to have some." I am indebted to former Secretary of Labor Ray Marshall for this account.

democratic societies. And again the resulting exercise of power is frequently viewed with grave alarm. The case of the trade union has already been cited. In the United States the right of the Communist party and its associated organizations to exist has been repeatedly challenged.[4] As has that of the Ku Klux Klan. And their rights have, of course, also been defended. The corporation is a creature of the state — in the United States of the individual state incorporation laws. As such, it enjoys full governmental protection. Its power, including that of the international or multinational enterprise, is also a source of worried comment and concern.

The dialectic of power as it is involved with the non-socialist state is, indeed, pervasively concerned with organizations.[5] They are protected; they are also subject to regulation and restraint. The vigor of the dialectic reflects the importance of organization as a source of power. A subversive individual is alarming and should be curbed; a subversive group is much worse. Governments are expected to suppress crime; it is especially important that they act against *organized* crime. On balance, however, organization as a source of power is far more protected than regulated. This, as we will see, has profound implications for the modern exercise of power, including both its concentration in a few great organizations and its diffusion to many lesser ones. But first the development and dynamics of power must be looked at in a larger perspective.

[4] Notably in the Smith Act of 1940.

[5] It is a pervasive issue also in the Communist world. There the dissident personality is a source of concern, but far more serious is the dissident organization. Lech Walesa was (and perhaps remains) a problem in Poland, but far more disturbing as a dialectical threat to the power of the state was Solidarity, the organization he headed.

X

The Larger Dynamics of Power
The Precapitalist World

HISTORY IS ORDINARILY written around the exercise of power — that by emperors and kings, the Church, dictators and democracies, generals and armies, capitalists and corporations. It could equally well be written around the sources of power and the instruments that enforce it. Historical change would then be the change in the relative roles of personality, property, and organization and of condign punishment, compensatory reward, and the explicit and implicit manifestations of conditioned power. History so written would not be without complexity. But there are broad contours evident in the rise of modern industrial society and in its antecedents that display the elements just mentioned. It is not with the history but with these contours that this and the following four chapters deal.

2

Power in Europe in precapitalist times — a convenient date[1] might be the beginning of the sixteenth century, immedi-

---

[1] The word *convenient* should be stressed. Merchant capitalism, or what is so designated, did not come suddenly or at a specific time to

ately following the first voyages of discovery to America and just prior to the preachings of Martin Luther — was divided broadly between the Church and the feudal baronage, with such authority as the latter might concede to the emerging central state. As to the sources of power, that of the Church derived from a superb organization sustained, in turn, by spacious and rich properties and by the conscientiously pictured and perpetuated personalities of Christ and the Supreme Being. This was, in the main, a conditioned exercise of power; people bent their will to that of the Church out of belief. The obedience so obtained covered both religious observances and requirements and secular action and behavior. The conditioning was both explicit and implicit. That the Church should be obeyed, its tenets accepted, was a conviction lodged deep in the culture of the age. It was what children accepted from their parents, what all in the community held to be both natural and proper. But the Church did not neglect more explicit conditioning; this was a major purpose of its large and remarkably sophisticated organization. To celebrate Mass and preach the gospel was to affirm and strengthen conditioned power, the instrument on which, more than any other, the power of the Church depended.

3

Social conditioning was not, however, the only instrument by which religious authority was enforced. Highly important was the income generated by the properties of the Church or received from and also demanded of its communicants. This supported priests, churches, and monas-

Italy, Spain, and northwestern Europe. It was a gradual development, with roots deep in the Middle Ages and even before.

teries;[2] such compensatory power was an effective and, indeed, indispensable buttress to the organization from which flowed the explicit conditioning.

Externally, the wealth of the Church also, if indirectly, sustained its influence. Churches and cathedrals were physical manifestations of its presence and authority. Then, as now, to be in a cathedral was to feel the presence of a power that it would seem wise to respect.

Compensatory power, as sufficiently noted, is generally associated with property. But here, as elsewhere, this was not exclusively so; perhaps the greatest single source of the power of the Church was its conditioned promise to the obedient of compensatory reward in the world to come. And this was notably specific, extending on to the quality and availability of the housing and urban amenities in the Heavenly City and the peace and abundant leisure of its inhabitants.

With social conditioning and its resulting belief and the associated compensatory power went a strongly persuasive use of condign power or the threat of its exercise. This embraced intensely painful and definitive punishment in this world and much worse in the hereafter. The physical chastisement and, as necessary, the summary dispatch of heretics were the approved designs for enforcement. On occasion, as in the case of the Inquisition, these achieved a high level of procedural dignity. More often, as in the pogroms in the Rhineland cities in the Middle Ages, they were merely the enthusiastic expression of faith of a highly conditioned populace. In the rather earlier case of the Cathars — the Albigensian heresy — who threatened substantial areas of the south of France in the twelfth and thirteenth centuries, the secular forces of the faithful nobles

[2] The recurrent and serious problem of simony is an indication of the way compensatory power supplemented conditioned obedience.

were commanded by Pope Innocent III to the aid of the Church in the condign task. This was carried through with energy and success. In 1245, when Montségur, a heretical center, was seized, some two hundred heretics were put to the stake, and a few years later condign chastisement was made policy for those still resisting churchly will in the papal bull of 1252, notably entitled *Ad extirpanda*.[3]

As a means of enforcing religious authority, the burning of dissenters and like manifestations of condign power against the living are much celebrated in religious history. (They are also only with some difficulty reconciled with the prominent role attributed to mercy in religious conditioning.) Without question, such enforcement was both unpleasant for the recipients and an impressive warning to potential recusants. It was, however, always much less important than the far more sophisticated promise of condign punishment or compensatory reward in the world to come. And while a certain moral stigma was always associated with the condign punishment of the living and with the cruelty involved, no comparable ill repute attached to the far more drastic and enduring punishment of the physically dead. In an age when life was almost always short and frequently unpleasant, the promise that something better and more lasting might follow was highly persuasive, as was the fear that things might be considerably worse. The general promise of eternal punishment or reward, the

---

[3] The essence of the heresy was a dualistic doctrine in which goodness exists only in a spiritual world, the material world being inherently evil. Among the more rigorous elements of lay obedience exacted by the Cathars, though not with complete success, was the prohibition of sexual intercourse. The heresy was especially objectionable, for it proceeded to organize its own priestly structure and church. Its suppression is thought to have served as a precedent for the Inquisition.

earthly acts of excommunication or bestowal of sacraments, were thus powerful condign or compensatory measures in support of conditioned obedience. Although in modern times the use of such punishment has declined substantially as a support to religious power, no one should be led, for that reason, to doubt its effectiveness in an earlier and devout, which is to say more effectively conditioned, society.

The external power of the Church — that over its communicants — was, as ever, the counterpart of its internal discipline and its internal exercise of power. Nothing, in consequence, was more important than a disciplined and obedient priesthood. The great crises in the power of the Church — the Avignon papacy and the Great Schism, the Reformation — came about because of internal division or indiscipline. The breakdown of internal power had a symmetrical external effect.

4

The basis of temporal power in precapitalist times does not lend itself as readily to characterization as does the much more sophisticated power of the Church, with which, on frequent occasion, it was in competition or in conflict.[4] The secular power was shared between the baronage — the feudal lords — and the emerging (and also competitive) nation-states. As between personality, property, and or-

---

[4] There have been times when the two were combined in the same person: one man united priestly and kingly authority. This has been notably true outside the Christian tradition in the cases of the Caliph, the Mikado, and Augustus as Pontifex Maximus. However, "at most times and places, the distinction between priest and king has been obvious and definite." Bertrand Russell, *Power: A New Social Analysis* (New York: W. W. Norton, 1938), pp. 50–51.

ganization, personality — the bold, sanguinary, and otherwise compelling leader — is the most celebrated in the conventional recording of history. Its importance is not in doubt, but there was a grave weakness involved: such personalities appeared, exerted influence, and then died or were killed; thus the temporal power based thereon rose and fell. This was in weak contrast with the continuing and immortal personality from which churchly power derived.

Property, on the other hand, was a durable source of temporal power in feudal times.[5] That possessed by the ruling lord allowed him to extend a living, more precisely the right to have a living, to a body of residents or retainers. The larger and more bountiful the property, the larger the number of such acolytes. The living so provided was the primitive counterpart of modern compensatory reward. It seems certain that on all feudal demesnes there was a lively instinct that any failure to accept the will of the feudal lord would have, along with its condign effects, some adverse economic consequences.

Finally, there was organization. This, it can safely be assumed, was a relatively slight source of feudal power. It was created ad hoc for military enterprises; little or nothing existed that could be considered a continuing administration. In India, where the feudal system survived into modern times, such organization as existed was the delegated responsibility of an often hereditary *dewan*. It was the persistent weakness, incompetence, and exactions of this system that made the British government frequently, indeed commonly, an attractive alternative.

[5] "The reason for the king's inability to govern without the barons was that the wealth and energy of the country were their private property." Bertrand de Jouvenel, *On Power: Its Nature and the History of Its Growth* (New York: Viking Press, 1949), p. 181, speaking of medieval France.

The feudal instruments of enforcement included the compensatory power already indicated and, without doubt, a good deal of explicit and implicit conditioning. The word of the feudal lord was meant to be accepted. So it had always been; the obligation was overtly emphasized day by day. Conditioned power was also borrowed from the Church: thus the divine right of kings and by extension of those who were subjects or rivals for their power. But pre-eminently, one must suppose, the principal instrument of enforcement in the feudal society was condign power. This was abundantly available for the punishment of those who inhabited the feudal lands. Symmetrically, it was the instrument by which external power was exerted. It was not by persuasion or purchase or even by marriage but by condign military action that the feudal lord sought to impose his will on those beyond his immediate territory.

5

The external power of the baronage depended extensively on the number of the feudal lord's internal subordinates, and their number was in direct proportion to the extent and quality of his landed property. For this reason virtually all feudal conflict, unless at religious behest, was over land.[6] To get land or more land was the immediate and obvious way of getting more feudatories, and with them more soldiers and thus more internal and external power. The result in Europe was nearly continuous territorial conflict between

[6] Religious purpose and pursuit of the power deriving from land and feudatories were anciently combined. Preaching the First Crusade in 1095, Urban II was at pains to observe that much good landed property would also be available for the taking in the redeemed Holy Land.

contenders for feudal power. Peace was an unstable equilibrium. Those most successful in the territorial struggle gradually established the larger suzerainty that became the nation-state. The territorial struggle within the baronage then transformed itself into a struggle between states. Intramural conflict over territory became international conflict.

The association between landed property, people, and power had a strong effect on political thought that endures to this day, even though the association itself has long since dissolved. Industrial property has replaced agricultural property as a source of revenue in support of internal power; crude manpower has ceased to be important as an instrument of external power. Land can be occupied and economic life will continue, but a modern industrial economy cannot be captured and still kept in working condition. Nonetheless, the notion that national power is enhanced by territorial acquisition continues to have a powerful hold on strategic and military thought. The modern military strategist looks at the map and assumes that any given land area is vulnerable to some adjacent power-aspiring aggressor. So it must have military defense. Because power was intimately associated in the now-distant past with productive acreage and the people who inhabited it, such acreage was an invitation to those seeking power. Thus it still appears to those who view things in a seemingly forthright and simple way.

The feudal sources and instruments of power — personality and landed property as the chief sources, condign enforcement as the major instrument — do not belong to an ancient and forgotten world. This expression of power survived into modern times in India, as we have seen, and also in Japan, China, and Imperial Russia. Remnants persist today in Central and South America, and the condign instruments that are invoked both in its defense and in opposition are the basis of much political turmoil in that part of the world.

But in the modern industrial society the feudal sources and instruments of power early surrendered primary place to a new combination, that associated with merchant and industrial capitalism. Not all that was before disappeared, but much that was new was added.

XI

The Emergence of Capitalism

IN WESTERN EUROPE in the two hundred and fifty years between the turn of the sixteenth century and the beginning of the Industrial Revolution in the second half of the eighteenth century, there was, notably in England and France, a progressive strengthening of the nation-state. This was in close descent from the traditional feudal exercise of power, with its source in landed property and personality and its reliance on condign power as well as on the compensatory resources deriving from the property and on the conditioned response to the sovereign with his frequent claim to divine right. But these years also saw the emergence, in varying importance, of a significant merchant class — the rise from yet earlier origins of merchant capitalism, as it has come to be known.[1]

This too can be seen, and is advantageously so seen, as a shift in the sources of power and in the instruments of its

---

[1] A development that was greatly diverse both as to the types of merchants involved and in the countries and cities where it occurred. On this I would commend the prodigious studies of the French historian Fernand Braudel, in particular *The Wheels of Commerce* (New York: Harper and Row, 1983).

enforcement. Merchant capitalism had its primary source of power in property, although this was no longer land but capital, notably goods for sale and the silver and gold for procuring them. Meanwhile, personality diminished in importance; organization became more evident. Compensatory power increased greatly; condign enforcement declined in use, although it was still available, and there was a limited but interesting exercise of conditioned power with portent for the future. It is one of the legitimate claims of capitalism that it substitutes more civilized compensatory reward for condign punishment; this was certainly true of merchant capitalism, at least as compared with the feudal exercise of power.

2

The names of the feudal lords, princes, and kings were much celebrated in their day; some still are. French and English history is a recital of their personal traits, eccentricities, and excesses and of the military campaigns by which they enlarged or defended the landed property that was the primary source of their power. The merchants, in contrast, were largely anonymous; they were not individuals but a class. Where one did emerge to popular recognition, he was, significantly, called a merchant prince.[2] He had acquired some of the feudal emphasis on personality. Certain personal qualifications — financial and commercial acumen, willingness to take risk, ability in assessing it, facility in recognizing opportunity, geographical and maritime knowledge — were important for success. But they were not adventitious and unique; they could be acquired and were. And they did not strongly suggest a capacity for leadership and command.

[2] Bankers, such as Jakob Fugger (1459–1525), were accorded similar feudal esteem.

The property that was the prime source of merchant power consisted of working capital — goods being transported or held for sale — as well as the ships that brought it to the merchants and the places of business in which it was sold.[3]

The merchants' capital also, and most significantly, included specie and in later times bank deposits. These were their claim on goods in trade. The aggregate of all the property of the merchant class was the source of its compensatory power. This won the submission of suppliers and servants and also, on occasion, of the feudal lords who tended to be notoriously in need of ready cash.[4] Property also accorded the merchants prestige in the community, which, in turn, won the conditioned submission that goes to wealth.

The primary exercise of power by the merchant capitalist was over the workers, artisans, and craftsmen whence came the goods, and over the quality and price of the goods that he sold, the most important being cloth,[5] and thus over the consumers who needed and purchased them. This, on first glance, was a relatively mild and benign exercise of power, for it left to both suppliers and consumers the alternative

[3] In the vicinity of Venice, Paris, and other cities, the merchants also came into possession of substantial landed estates. These were, it seems fairly certain, subsidiary to their main business property.

[4] The discovery of America with the resulting large flow of precious metals to Europe — silver, in the main, and not gold as commonly assumed — has frequently been thought a decisive new source of capital and a factor in the rise of merchant capitalism. It was not unimportant, but it reflects a common misunderstanding of the nature of capital. The inflow of metal provided an abundant means of exchange. It set in motion an enduring inflation, which may well have been encouraging to trade. For the individual merchant it was a claim on the capital of others. It did not, however, directly enlarge the total stock of goods in process of manufacture or being held for sale or the tools and equipment for manufacture or the facilities for transport or sale. These, then as now, were the real capital.

[5] With food and shelter, one of the three universally needed consumption goods of the age.

of not producing or buying or of seeking out other sellers or buyers. However, need for a market and a livelihood and for a product can be compelling, and it was a prime feature of merchant capitalism that it provided careful safeguards against a promiscuous resort to alternative buyers or sources of supply. The power of any merchant could be sadly reduced were another to offer more for a product of given quality or offer to sell one for less. Competition was seriously adverse to merchant success. To ensure against it, organization became significant as a source of power.

The great merchants lived in relatively close urban association. It was a simple and obvious step to enhance their compensatory power by a close regulation of quality and prices both when buying and selling. In earlier times this had been the service of the merchant guilds, but by this time they were somewhat in decline in Western Europe. Craft guilds controlling the prices and quality of goods by and for sellers had invaded and challenged their power. Again the symmetrical response. But the merchants had another major source of support and a major defense against competition. This was the emerging state, which protected them against competition, especially from foreign sources, and undertook the regulation of trade in general. Organization, that of the state, thus became a source of power alongside property; and its service to merchant capitalism was deemed an act of public virtue. This social conditioning was the service of the mercantilist philosophers, on which, presently, I will also have a word. Unrestricted competition did not achieve its reputation as a major public good until the different circumstances of manufacturers following the Industrial Revolution made freedom from craft-guild and government restraint a preferable alternative. Then, as ever, the ideas — the social conditioning — were brought abreast of the need.

3

In the great merchant cities — Venice, Bruges, Amsterdam in considerable measure, and others — the merchant interest and that of the government of the city were coterminous. There could be no serious tension between the merchants and the state; essentially they were the same. Elsewhere the merchants were in frequently uneasy association with the feudal ruling classes, which is to say merchant property as a source of power was in competition with that deriving extensively from landed property. The compensatory power of the merchants was in continuing competition with the conditioned power that associated government as a matter of course with the landed property of the feudal classes. This latter expression of conditioned power was exceedingly durable. In England until comparatively recent times, the landed aristocracy was referred to, automatically, as the ruling class; theirs was the conditioned right to power. Merchants, in contrast, suffered the derogatory and occasionally derisory reference of being "in trade." There was, as well, an uneasy association between the merchants and the Church. Even in Catholic cities the merchants were, on occasion, casual about the social conditioning of the Church and on some matters, such as the taking of interest, openly adverse. Also the merchant cities and cities with large merchant enclaves such as London and Amsterdam were, partly because of the lenient attitude toward religious conditioning, extensively a haven for Jews, Huguenots, and diverse recusants.[6]

[6] There was, as well, a progressive reduction in the scope of religious exercise. On this R. H. Tawney has a notable comment: ". . . side by side with the expansion of trade and the rise of new

The late sixteenth, seventeenth, and early eighteenth centuries were, nonetheless, a time of steadily growing power for the merchants as compared with their rival claimants. Capital as a form of property was a less visible but a more mobile and adaptable source of power than land. And from it and the associated organization came a new and effective exercise of conditioned power.

This was the contribution of the mercantilist philosophers earlier mentioned. Thomas Mun, himself a London merchant, in his posthumous *Discourse on England's Treasure by Forraign Trade* (1664), Sir James Steuart, the last of the great British mercantilists, Jean Baptiste Colbert (1619–1683) at the more practical level in France, and others all strongly identified the merchant's interest in increasing his own stock of precious metals with that of the nation-state; what served the merchant's interest served the wealth and power of the state. Nothing else was so important. From this belief, in turn, came a policy of encouraging exports, taxing, restricting, or otherwise discouraging imports and therewith foreign competition[7] and (notably in the case of Colbert) providing detailed regulation of other aspects of trade. In this fashion the needs of the merchants were reflected through social conditioning in the approved policies of the state. It is not to be supposed that many read or knew of the mercantilist doctrine at the time.

---

classes to political power . . . was the contraction of the territory within which the writ of religion was conceived to run. The criticism which dismisses the concern of Churches with economic relations and social organization as a modern innovation finds little support in past history. What requires explanation is not the view that these matters are part of the province of religion, but the view that they are not." *Religion and the Rise of Capitalism* (Harmondsworth, Eng.: Penguin Books, 1972), p. 272.

[7] Other mercantilists, especially Sir William Petty (1623–1687) and Sir Dudley North (1641–1691), relented on protection and argued the possibilities and advantages of uninhibited trade.

And it was undoubtedly a slight thing when compared with the social conditioning that came to the support of industrial capitalism in later years. But it was highly influential with those whose actions — regulation of foreign trade and of imports in particular, grants of exclusive trading areas, maintenance of ports and harbors — served the merchants' power and interest.

4

For conduct of business in a city or a limited trading area, the merchant's enterprise was, in greater or less degree of organization, sufficient. For overseas operations — the procurement and sale of goods at a great distance in primitive or culturally different lands — something more formidable was required. Accordingly, at the beginning of the seventeenth century there came into being the greatest organizational achievement of merchant capitalism, the chartered companies. Originally temporary groupings of merchants for a particular voyage or expedition, these companies soon developed a solid and sophisticated structure. In accordance with mercantilist doctrine, they were granted a monopoly of the trade in the regions into which they entered. They were also endowed with something approaching immortality. The East India Company — the Governor and Company of Merchants of London, trading into the East Indies — was chartered by Elizabeth I on the last day of the year 1600 and survived for the next 274 years; the Hudson's Bay Company, more imaginatively styled the Governor and Company of Adventurers of England, trading into Hudson's Bay, received its charter from Charles II in 1670 and, of course, still exists. It is one of the weaknesses of personality as a source of power that it is subject to the limitations of the human life span. This the Church had overcome through organization. Now the chartered company, and later the corporation, overcame this considerable defect by the same means. Although in the history of the great chartered companies the names of a few persons emerge — John Smith of the London Company and the Virginia settlement, Robert Clive and Warren Hastings of the East India Company — this was the beginning of a movement, long to be continued under capitalism, away from personality as a source of power. The final manifestation would be in the modern corporation, the lineal descendant of the chartered company.

Chartered companies appeared because stronger organization was necessary as a source of continuing power. The merchants also needed access to condign measures in order to protect shipping, to pacify and otherwise occupy the trading areas into which they moved (and, of course, to resist the intrusion of competing companies). Thus endowed with access to condign power, including the right to hire, deploy, and use soldiery, the chartered companies had the principal attributes of a nation-state. And this in India, the Dutch East Indies, and the vast reaches of northern North America they became.

It was their singular advantage that, almost everywhere, they moved into what rather precisely could be called a power vacuum. The term, though rarely if ever defined in modern usage, aptly describes a community or territory where all the sources of power — effective personality, property, and organization — are feeble or absent, as also, in consequence, are all the instruments of its enforcement. This accurately describes the East Indies and the subarctic reaches of North America as they were invaded by the trading companies. In northern America there was, in these terms, nearly nothing; in the East Indies there were occasional personalities, some property, and some slight organization. But these, and especially the organization, were weak compared with those possessed by the Europeans, and so were the resulting instruments of enforcement.

In time, and more specifically in the last century, the trading companies gave way, in their overseas operations, to formal extensions of the originating state. Company operations became colonies; power now traced to the colonial government and its revenue resources and, on occasion, as in the later example of Cecil Rhodes in Africa, to a particularly expressive personality. Or, as in the important case of China, nominal independence was subject to the power deriving from the property and organization of the merchants who had access, as in the Opium Wars, to the condign power of their country of origin. With these changes the merchant power was also diluted. Imperial power was pursued, in part, for its own sake. There was land to be taken up, notably in the Americas, with the income and the compensatory power that went with its possession. And there were souls to be rescued and added to those already within the fold of what is rightly called organized religion. In many of the colonial lands, especially in Latin America, the power proceeding from landed property (including that of the Catholic Church as a large proprietor) much exceeded that of the merchants. In Mexico when the revolt came, it was not against the merchants but against the great landowners, including the Church.

5

In Europe, the eighteenth century may be marked as the high tide of merchant capitalism. By the turn of the next century, so great were its prestige and the impression of power it conveyed that Napoleon's Berlin and Milan Decrees,

England's answering Orders in Council, and the resulting restrictions on trade were considered major strategic moves in the Napoleonic struggles and ever since have enjoyed a reputation which is not deserved.[8] Already, however, a great change was in progress, involving a sizable invasion of merchant power. This was the Industrial Revolution and the development of industrial capitalism.

Few matters have been more debated by historians than the nature and sources of the Industrial Revolution. Was it brought about in the latter half of the eighteenth century by the more or less accidental appearance of a particularly imaginative and inventive group of entrepreneurs — the two Abraham Darbys, John Kay, James Hargreaves, Richard Arkwright, and James Watt? Or was it the product of a largely independent process of technological advance that brought with it the making of pig iron with coal, steam power from the same fuel, and, above all, the application of power to the mechanical spinning and weaving of textiles? Had it not been Arkwright, Hargreaves, and the rest, would it not have been someone else? Was it not a historically scheduled step in the general march of technology — and of capitalism?

What is not in doubt is that the Industrial Revolution involved a large, even spectacular, shift in the sources of power and, in lesser measure, in the instruments of its enforcement. Property remained central as a source of power; there was, however, another dramatic change in its character. It was no longer the stock-in-trade and other working capital of the merchant but the fixed assets — mills, fac-

---

[8] These were pioneer exercises in the imposition of sanctions. In the official mind sanctions remain an instrument of great effect; only after they are imposed is it learned that they are rather easily suffered and with slight effort evaded. Substitutes and substitute sources of supply abound. This lesson is thereafter soon forgotten.

tories, machinery — of the industrial capitalist. With the change in the nature of the property involved went another in the nature of the organization. The merchant had obtained his product from independent or self-employed craftsmen, artisans, and other workers in a relatively loose compensatory arrangement. The workers were now brought directly into the mill towns and the factories, which allowed of a far stronger exercise of compensatory power over those who made the product.

Conventional historiography also accords a much-enhanced role to personality. With the Industrial Revolution the entrepreneur — independent, innovative, imaginative, resourceful, sometimes ruthless, always intelligent — became a key figure on the economic scene. Perhaps so. But, as always, there must be a word of caution. Personality as a source of power is wonderfully attractive to the more susceptible historian as, in modern times, to the more impressionable journalist. Industrial capitalism owed its strength, in fact, to its access to all three sources of power — to property in mill, machinery, and working capital; to a greatly advanced form of organization binding workers to the industrial firm; and, of course, to the entrepreneurial personality.

As to the instruments of enforcement, condign power continued in decline. It was available by purchase or gift from the state and used as necessary against troublemakers, those who might try to organize workingmen's associations or unions or who were otherwise disposed to unduly expressed discontent. Mostly, however, submission was won by compensatory power. A long-persisting myth held that the workers who were now gathered into town and factory from the villages and from the cottage industries by which they and their parents had been sustained were subject to an especially oppressive power by the new industrial capitalists. The force of that power — the degree of submission demanded — cannot be doubted; we recall again that at the minimum levels of compensatory power, with starvation as the alternative, the difference from condign power is not great. But the cottage industries pursued on behalf of the merchants — the spinning and weaving from early morning until late at night and always under the threat of painful deprivation — had also been harsh in their discipline. Employers can exploit workers, but workers under pressure of stark and painful need can exploit themselves.[9] Men and women had come to the factories from the feudal estates as well. There, too, the laborer's existence was narrow, a submission in response to small compensatory reward, the traditional conditioned power of the landlord and at least the memory of his ability to inflict condign punishment. The predominantly compensatory power of early industrial capitalism was not a pleasant thing for those subject to it; it is not clear that it was more stern and demanding than what had gone before.

[9] "[E]xploitation is more shameless in the so-called domestic industry than in manufactures, and that because the power of resistance in the labourers decreases with their dissemination, because a whole series of plundering parasites insinuate themselves between the employer and the workman . . ." Karl Marx, *Capital* (New York: International Publishers, 1967), p. 462.

XII

The Power of High Capitalism

WITH THE INDUSTRIAL REVOLUTION and the great movement in the sources of power from the working capital of the merchants to the hard industrial capital of the industrialists came a marked advance in organization. A tightly organized labor force held together by wages replaced the near and distant suppliers of goods held together only by the act of purchase. There was movement from the (possibly) more anonymous merchant to the more clearly recognizable personality of the industrial entrepreneur. As with the merchants, compensatory power was the dominant instrument for winning submission. But there was also now a new and important deployment of conditioned power, which radically altered the beliefs that governed economic action by the state. Reflecting these beliefs, the state grew greatly sympathetic to the needs and desires of the industrialists; it became, in substantial measure, an extension of their arm. In time, this conditioning also altered the way people led their lives and pursued their happiness. The approved mode of life became subordinate to the purposes of industry; it came to serve industrial power. The conditioned power of industrial capitalism as it developed and grew effective in the nineteenth century would remain an influential instrument of power for generations to come. As would the massive countervailing response that it occasioned.

The primary author of this social conditioning was Adam Smith; rarely in history has there been such complete agreement on the intellectual role of a single figure. Others would contribute much; Smith's name would remain pre-eminent. Leading the opposition as the architect of the countering belief three quarters of a century later was the equally compelling figure of Karl Marx.

2

The contribution of Adam Smith to the social conditioning of industrial capitalism came in *The Wealth of Nations*,[1] published in the year of the declaration of American independence, 1776. That the two events occurred at the same time was not entirely coincidence; the book and the Revolution were in similar reaction to the constraints of merchant capitalism.[2]

Smith's contribution was both negative and affirmative, an attack on the ideological sources of merchant power and an affirmation of what served the emergent industrialists. The industrialists, though still in a primitive state of de-

[1] More specifically, *An Inquiry into the Nature and Causes of the Wealth of Nations*.

[2] The American merchants who "when their interests were jeopardized . . . entered politics with a vim, and might be expected to carry things their own way" had trading interests in conflict with English regulation and protection. They were not, however, unambiguously in opposition to British rule. See Arthur Meier Schlesinger (Sr.), *The Colonial Merchants and the American Revolution, 1763–1776* (New York: Frederick Ungar, 1966). Quotation on page 29.

velopment when Smith wrote, were already enjoying large cost advantages as compared with household industry. This Smith saw, although he attributed it less to the new machinery than to the breaking up of the industrial tasks in the factory and the application of specialized skill and effort to each of the parts. The gains from this division of labor led to regional and national specialization in production and became the case for freedom of internal and international trade. Standing in the way and in need of being dismantled was the protective and regulatory apparatus of merchant capitalism. The removal of regulations and restraints on trade reflected the interest of the industrialist; with his lower costs he had everything to gain from the freedom to undersell the local merchants. Were he an English or Scottish manufacturer, he was well ahead in industrial development and so had little to fear from the competition of like producers in other countries and everything to gain from a principle that defended his access to their markets.[3]

On a yet broader plane, Smith identified the pursuit of all economic self-interest with the public good. The businessman so motivated "intends only his own gain, and he is in this, as in many other cases, led by an invisible hand to promote an end which was no part of his intention."[4] It would be hard to imagine an idea more serviceable to industrial power, and none, indeed, has served so long. The industrialist had no need to present himself as a public benefactor; this would have been sadly unconvincing in any

[3] Smith went on to prescribe close limits on other activities of the state, and notably those that would be at cost in taxation to the industrialist.

[4] Adam Smith, *The Wealth of Nations* (Chicago: University of Chicago Press, 1976), Book I, p. 477. The invisible hand is a metaphor. Smith, a man of the Enlightenment, did not ascribe supernatural support to the pursuit of business gain. Not all of his followers have been so restrained.

case.[5] Virtue was given to his actions by an overriding law to which he, however selfish or sordid his purposes or motivations, was wholly subject.

Smith was not completely at the service of industrial capitalism and certainly not durably so. In keeping with his antimercantilist position, he had grave doubts about the great chartered companies and, by implication, the corporations in descent therefrom. Modern corporate executives pay an obeisance to Smith that he would not return. Troublesome also was his opposition to monopoly, that of the individual firm or of a conspiracy between firms. Competition was a needed brake on industrial power, but in Smith's view it existed in unstable equilibrium. No one accepted it if it could be constrained or avoided.[6] Once competition was lost, the invisible hand was withdrawn. This qualification would be a source of considerable inconvenience in the next two hundred years, especially in the United States. Great corporations, sheltering behind the invisible hand, would have to assert, in face of grievously adverse evidence, that the requisite competition still prevailed.

Much of the strength of Smith's social conditioning is to be attributed to his stubborn unwillingness to make concessions to those whose power he sustained and enlarged. He was manifestly an independent man; and no one could suppose he was the creature of those whose interests he served, whose conditioning he provided.[7] The condition-

[5] Smith himself made the point: "I have never known much good done by those who affected to trade for the public good." Smith, *Wealth of Nations*, Book I, p. 478.

[6] This was the thrust of his most frequently quoted sentence: "People of the same trade seldom meet together, even for merriement and diversion, but the conversation ends in a conspiracy against the public, or in some contrivance to raise prices." Smith, *Wealth of Nations*, Book I, p. 144.

[7] Reaction to Smith's persuasion was prompt. A year and a half after Smith's death in 1790, William Pitt the younger, in introducing

ing that served the industrial power was not necessarily either contrived or visibly sycophantic. But its service to economic interest was, nonetheless, the test of its acceptability.

3

In the hundred years and more following the publication of *The Wealth of Nations* the sources and instruments of capitalist power were much strengthened. In the United States, spectacular and highly motivated personalities — Vanderbilt, Gould, Rockefeller, Harriman, Carnegie, Frick, Morgan, and others — moved onto the scene, and their somewhat less conspicuous counterparts appeared in Britain, France, and Germany. An increasingly close association developed between those who founded and ran the great industrial enterprises, now including the railroads, and those (like Morgan) who supplied them with money capital for the creation or, more often, the acquisition and combination of those enterprises.

Supporting the personalities of the great entrepreneurs was the massive aggregation of property they commanded. This, too, was a highly important, highly visible source of power. And as the nineteenth century was ending, industrial organization became increasingly important. Already in the last half of that century, as Alfred D. Chandler, Jr., has

---

his budget, said of him that his "extensive knowledge of detail and depth of philosophical research will, I believe, furnish the best solution of every question connected with the history of commerce and with the system of political economy." Address before the House of Commons on February 17, 1792, quoted in John Rae, *Life of Adam Smith* (New York: Augustus M. Kelley, 1965), pp. 290–91. This is a notable tribute to the exercise of conditioned power.

pointed out,[8] the corporation was ceasing to be the extended arm of the boss at the top. It was coming to be governed by the administrative structure embracing varied specialists and technicians that was eventually to be called *the* management. Organization was emerging as a source of power in industrial capitalism; eventually it would replace property as the dominant source of such power.

With the changes in the sources of power went changes in the instruments of enforcement. Condign power did not disappear; it remained available from the state or from company police. But it was of small importance as compared with the massive deployment of compensatory power. This was most evident in all the industrial countries, where millions of workers were mobilized in the service of the industrial system. And it was also apparent in the less astringent power of producers over consumers, a submission that earlier, as in the cases of Rockefeller over the users of kerosene and of Vanderbilt and the railroads over shippers of products, had been severe. Compensatory power extended to the purchase of legislators and other public officials and thus to winning the support of the instruments of the power of the state. In the latter years of the last century the United States Senate was commonly referred to as a rich man's club; this is another way of saying that it was the well-paid instrument of the capitalist age.

However, the most interesting and, quite possibly, the most important achievement of high capitalism was its continuing resort to conditioned power — its continuing accommodation of economic ideas to current need and reality. Much of this conditioning was still of British origin; it was a service in which, until modern times, Britain was pre-eminent. It attracted the efforts of a notable succession

[8] *The Visible Hand: The Managerial Revolution in American Business* (Cambridge: Harvard University Press, 1977), pp. 81–121.

of scholars who refined and enlarged the earlier Smithian principles. All, in one way or another, produced ideas that were in support of the submission that served the power of the industrialists.

Thus, in the early industrial establishments, the wages of the workers were minute as compared with the employers' return. No one could doubt that the system treated different participants in radically different ways, and the contrast was heightened by the circumstance that the industrial capitalist, rather more than his merchant predecessor, lived in fairly close juxtaposition to his workers. Inequality, the difference in living standard as it would now be called, was dramatically visible. The requisite social conditioning to make this acceptable came in an extraordinarily telling way in the writings of two highly influential figures, David Ricardo (1772–1823) and Thomas Robert Malthus (1766–1834), contemporaries and friends, who united in attributing the low wages and the resulting inequality to the prodigious and devastating fertility of the working classes; it was their uninhibited breeding that was the cause of their poverty. This kept wages at subsistence levels — the equilibrium to which, from the force of numbers, they tended. Ricardo called this the iron law of wages. Not the iniquitous industrial capitalist, not the system, but the worker himself was the architect of his own misery.[9]

To the conditioning of Ricardo and Malthus were added the views of the utilitarians, whose most articulate and compelling voice was that of Jeremy Bentham (1748–1832).

---

[9] For Ricardo the worker also suffered from the still-surviving landed interest. "The interest of the landlord is always opposed to that of the consumer and manufacturer." *Principles of Political Economy and Taxation* (London: Everyman Edition, 1926), p. 225. As quoted in Eric Roll, *A History of Economic Thought*, rev. ed. (New York: Prentice-Hall, 1942), p. 198.

Bentham and his followers urged the testing of all public action by the rule "The greatest good for the greatest number." The policy that best served this end was one of laissez-faire. The freedom of the industrialist to follow his own interest thus became a matter of high social principle. The result might not be perfect, but it was the best possible. Implicit and, in some measure, explicit was the idea that not all could prosper; some must fall by the wayside in order that the greatest number be served. Suffering and deprivation were inevitable even in this best of all possible worlds.

There was more yet to come, and it came in the latter half of the century in England with Herbert Spencer (1820–1903), whose words echoed strongly across the Atlantic. In works of impressive scholarship, Spencer made the ultimate case for industrial capitalism: it was the manifestation of Darwin in the social order; its governing principle was the survival of the fittest. The great industrial capitalists, as they now were, were great because they were biologically superior; the poor were poor because they were inferior. Wealth was the reward of those who were inherently better; the effort to attain it both revealed and developed that superiority. The poverty of the poor was now seen to be socially good; it contributed to the euthanasia of the weakest elements of the society. William Graham Sumner (1840–1910) of Yale, the most resonant American economic voice of the time, extended Spencer's influence in the United States. So, if less formally, did Henry Ward Beecher (1813–1887) — "God intended the great to be great and the little to be little."

There was also the important service of the economic hedonists and the associated marginalists. The hedonists, best represented in the writings of William Stanley Jevons

(1835–1882), held that the enduring and comprehensive aim of man was always to maximize pleasure, minimize pain. To this end the service of goods, their utility, was central. So, accordingly, was that of the industrialist who provided them. Jevons also supplied the rationale for the principal calculation relating to human welfare, the adjustment of purchases so that each was extended to the point where pleasure or, in any case, satisfaction was the same — was equalized at the margin. The precision of this exercise, it followed, and not the prices or performance of the industrialist, was what was important to human well-being.

Further, and enduring, conditioning came from the great Italian sociologist and economist Vilfredo Pareto (1848–1923), who dealt explicitly with the inequality in the distribution of income under high capitalism. This unequal distribution, he determined, was a constant in different industrial countries at different times. And he went on to conclude that this "constancy of inequality in the distribution of income reflects inequality of human ability, which is a natural and universal category."[10]

Given the starkly visible inequality under high capitalism, the serviceability of this conclusion will also be evident. Traces of Pareto's "law" endured for many decades in economic instruction.[11]

---

[10] As quoted in Roll, *History of Economic Thought*, p. 453.

[11] Not all of the conditioning in support of high capitalism served. Thus an engaging line of argument justified the return to capital and therefore to the capitalist as the reward for abstinence — for refraining from consumption. The abstinence theories of capital enjoyed a not wholly insignificant place in economic thought in the nineteenth century and early in the twentieth. They were, alas, rather obtrusively inconsistent with the style of living of the great capitalists, a style that made it hard to suggest that their self-denial had been so painful as to require reward.

4

With all of the foregoing went the continuing celebration of the market. Not only did its uninhibited operation accord the greatest good to the greatest number, but it was also an effective solvent — and concealment — of the power of industrial capitalism. Prices were set by the market. Wages were set by the market. So were the prices of all the other requisites of production. Production decisions were in response to the market. On none of these matters did the industrialist have power; hence there could be no legitimate concern as to its exercise. Only those insufficiently instructed in the nature of the market could believe his power to exist. Here was the supreme conditioning achievement of what has come to be called classical economics. It guided the power of the industrialist, however against his intention, to good social ends; it also denied the existence of such power. And it taught this to all who sought to understand the workings of the system.[12] This instruction, needless to say, still

[12] The social conditioning of high capitalism, it should be noticed, was adjusted to national need. England, including southern Scotland, had a large head start in industrial development. Free entry of manufactures into other markets was much to be desired; protection, particularly on food grains, raised the cost of living and thus the cost of home labor. American, German, and French industrialists, coming later on the scene, needed protection from the British imports. Accordingly, in the United States, Germany, and France, the classical ideas on trade were amended to embrace a needed component of tariff protection. Henry Charles Carey (1793–1879), the most influential American economist of the last century, and Friedrich List (1789–1846), his counterpart in Germany, wrote eloquently and effectively on the desirability of protective tariffs; free trade was an impractical and damaging policy. In the United States and Germany the ideas of Carey and List were thought highly reputable and greatly approved.

persists. Nothing is so important in the defense of the modern corporation as the argument that its power does not exist — that all power is surrendered to the impersonal play of the market, all decision is in response to the instruction of the market. And nothing is more serviceable than the resulting conditioning of the young to that belief.

XIII

The Response

WE HAVE SEEN that any exercise of power produces a generally similar and opposite exercise. So with the power of high capitalism. The response it induced began in the middle of the last century, although it had earlier manifestations. It centered not on the comparatively mild submission of consumers of the products of industrial capitalism (although, as railroad users, oil buyers, and others, they were heard from) but on the much more comprehensive, much more onerous submission required of its workers. Its sources were in personality and organization. The personality was that of Karl Marx, aided, abetted, and financed by his lifelong friend Friedrich Engels. The organization lay in the Workingmen's Association of 1864, usually called the First International, the parent of a great number of lesser and later groups.

As to the instruments of enforcement of the Marxist revolt: there was no appreciable continuing emphasis on condign power, but it would, of course, be required for the overthrow of capitalism in its last attenuated days. Nor was any compensatory power immediately involved; that would, instead, be the reward of the better times after the revolution. Overwhelmingly, the Marxist instrument was conditioned power to the near exclusion of both of the other means of enforcement. It was to this that Marx devoted himself over a lifetime, as did his followers. His writings — *Capital, The Communist Manifesto*, and numerous lesser tracts — were the text even as the Bible and the Quran were for the religiously committed. From these works, in thousands of speeches, meetings, study groups, and union halls, came the instruction by his acolytes. As an exercise of power, it paralleled and, in many respects, rivaled that of the Church itself. Attacking property as a source of power, Marx showed, as no secular figure had before, how social conditioning could be an instrument for exercising power.[1]

2

Marx's use of conditioned power came to bear symmetrically on the classical economists who were the source of the conditioned power of industrial capitalism and also — a point of major Marxist emphasis — on the financial integument by which capitalist purpose was united. He accepted a basic tenet earlier postulated by Smith and Ricardo: goods have value in proportion to the labor incorporated therein — the labor theory of value. But it was Marx's case that only a fraction of this value was returned to the worker in his wages; surplus value in the form of interest, profits, and rents was appropriated by the capitalist. Wages were kept low by the pressure of unemployment — by the omnipresent industrial reserve army in urgent need of work. Should

---

[1] Of this Marx himself was certain. "In every epoch, the ruling ideas have been the ideas of the ruling class." Karl Marx and Friedrich Engels, *The Communist Manifesto*.

wages rise because of an unnatural scarcity of workers, this would provoke a crisis, in modern language a depression. Such crises, occurring with ever-increasing severity, would ultimately bring an end to capitalist power. Also inducing to the demise would be the great process of capitalist concentration: large capitalists would gobble up the smaller businessmen or force them into the proletariat. Not the competition of the classical economists but the monopoly they deplored was on the wave of the future. Along with the crises, attenuation and weakness from the concentration would contribute to the final collapse. While the system would fall largely of its own incompetent weight, Marx did not exclude some exercise of condign power — revolutionary action — when the day came.

Seeing the contemporary state as the instrument of capitalist power — "an executive committee for managing the affairs of the governing class as a whole" — Marx naturally saw the postrevolutionary government as the instrument of the now-triumphant workers, the workers' state. In that state, needless to say, workers would enjoy the full fruits of their labor. The organization that would make this possible remained, perhaps conveniently, obscure. Had the bureaucratic structure that would be required been fully envisaged, it would have cost something in approval.[2]

3

All of the above, and of course much more, passed from the pen of Marx into the conditioned belief that sustained his

[2] A point on which Joseph Schumpeter was prescient. "I for one cannot visualize, in the conditions of modern society, a socialist organization in any form other than that of a huge and all-embracing bureaucratic apparatus." *Capitalism, Socialism, and Democracy,* 2nd ed. (New York: Harper and Brothers, 1947), p. 206.

power. It was and remains an extraordinary achievement. For a century and more after it was written, it would capture the minds and thus the submission of millions. And there would be testament to its effectiveness from those who dissapproved of and feared it. Marxist propaganda — social conditioning by Marx and his followers — became synonymous with massive evil. Marxist teaching in colleges and universities and Marxist books in libraries invited deep concern as instruments of his power. Those who voiced his ideas were kept on the social fringe; they were not to be trusted with grave public or private responsibility. As Marx rightly sensed the force of the conditioned power he challenged, so equally those who resisted him sensed his power.

4

Great as it was and great as was the fear that it aroused, Marxist power failed everywhere in the industrialized countries in face of the normal manifestation of industrial capitalist power. The latter, combining property and organization as sources of power with a strong deployment of compensatory and its own conditioned power, was too strong. The Marxist success came in the largely or wholly preindustrial communities of Russia and China,[3] where it was aided by the breakdown of the preindustrial state as the result of war and internal conflict. In both cases Marxist organization and social conditioning moved into a power vacuum — a context in which personality, property, and organization had dissolved as sources of power and condign, compensatory, and conditioned instruments of its enforcement had become nugatory or largely so.

Though Marx did not succeed in any practical way in

[3] As, in very marginal fashion, in Africa and also in Cuba.

Western Europe or Japan, his social conditioning was deep and enduring there. He was not as influential in Britain, where a less strenuous parliamentary socialism captured the anticapitalist response. And he had but slight effect among American workers. Once again the reasons are evident when the corpus of power is dissected. Marx, as a personality, was distant from the United States, far from being evocative to the American worker. The Marxist organization did not extend effectively across the Atlantic. Most of all, the social conditioning, which was superbly relevant to Europe, was much less so in the United States, where property was more widely possessed and wages were higher. Also, the American worker did not see his own submission to his employer as inevitable; he could escape to another job or, on occasion, to the frontier. His government, however subject to the needs of industrial capitalism, also conveyed a greater impression of accessibility to the individual than did the governments of Europe. It is at least possible, as well, that American workers were intellectually more immune to the social conditioning of economic and political thought than were their European counterparts. It was not part of their everyday discussion or prominent in their reading or education.

None of this is to say that the power of industrial capitalism in the United States failed to produce a countervailing effort. As the nineteenth century passed, the smaller property owners, particularly the farmers, found themselves in increasing opposition to the industrialists and more especially their financial allies, who were thought to be exercising their power to keep farm prices low and costs, including the cost of money, high. This produced the social conditioning — the countering agitation, particularly against the financial interests — that extended from Andrew Jackson to William Jennings Bryan. For the working classes the

Knights of Labor and the IWW (Industrial Workers of the World) also gave brief but vigorous expression to worker dissent. However, neither the agrarian nor the proletarian response succeeded in face of the vastly superior deployment of the various elements of industrial and financial power.

At the end of the century, Thorstein Veblen ridiculed the social observances and folk rites of the industrial rich with superb skill. In the years following, the muckrakers celebrated the avarice, cupidity, and, needless to say, the abuse of power by the capitalists. This, too, achieved a certain conditioned belief but was never a serious threat.

A more articulate and durable reaction to industrial power in the United States came not from Marx but from within the body of classical economics itself. According to its doctrine, capitalist power was to be countered by the operation of competition and the market; it was to be firmly in the service of the public, whatever the intention of its possessor might be. The dissenting response to industrial power in the United States accepted that all this was so; it was only that monopolies, highly visible in steel, oil, tobacco, and the railroads, were in palpable conflict with the competitive ideal. The answer to the power so asserted was to restore competition in those industries or, were that impossible, to provide suitable regulation. Thus the response to industrial capitalist power took the form of proposals for breaking up the great trusts, for the passage of legislation to this effect, and for regulation of the railroads. It was not without result. It brought the passage of the Interstate Commerce Act in 1887, the Sherman Antitrust Act three years later, and the Clayton Antitrust and Federal Trade Commission acts in the administration of Woodrow Wilson. In all of these actions those reacting to industrial power accepted the basic premises of industrial capitalist conditioning. The beneficence of the market was not in doubt; it was only necessary that policy recognize and act where the premises did not hold.

It was also, as regards the power of industrial capitalism, a largely harmless response. Enforcement of the antitrust laws involved much cherished employment and revenue for lawyers and some inconvenience and cost to those whose power was so challenged. It had, however, a negligible effect on industrial development, including competition, and thus on the relevant source of industrial power. (There was no perceptible difference in the industrial development and resulting concentration in the United States, where it was policy to promote competition, and in Europe, where no such effort was made.) At the same time, the emotion and effort of those who reacted to industrial power were channeled harmlessly into demands and hopes that the antitrust laws might be enforced — a hope that, transcending all experience, is not yet quite dead. And even those most opposed to industrial power could continue to instruct the young in the desirability of market competition and in the prospect that one day it would be achieved. Had industrial capitalism designed the conditioned response to its own power, it could scarcely have done better.

5

A final word is necessary on the role and power of the state in the age of high capitalism. Marx's deathless observation that the state is the executive committee of the governing classes owes more to its brilliantly articulated core of truth than to its precise description of the reality. The power of the state — its laws and their condign enforcement, its compensatory power, as, for example, in the land grants to the American and Canadian railroads, and its general social conditioning through education and the reiteration of the conventional wisdom on the values of work, obedience, self-help, decent frugality, and much more — was exercised on behalf of the industrial power and very often at its behest. The state was an extension of the instruments of enforcement of industrial capitalism; it did for industrial capitalism what industrial capitalism could not do for itself. That the United States government or that of Britain might be regarded as an enemy of business, a commonplace conception today, would not have entered anyone's mind in the middle of the last century.

But to assign the nineteenth-century state exclusively to the service of high industrial capitalism would also be wrong. Individual citizens with their privilege of the franchise had a similar claim on the powers of the government. The state protected persons as well as property; and, in a primitive way, it could be called on to protect persons from the depredations of the possessors of property. And other interests — farmers, small businessmen, religious groups, in some industrial countries the old landed classes — had a certain access to government power.

Nor was all state power exercised on behalf of or at the behest of others. Reaching back to its own sources — its evocative personalities (Presidents, prime ministers, other politicians), its property, and its developing organization — government also deployed condign, compensatory, and conditioned power for its own purposes. Tendencies were present, notably in organization, that, in the twentieth century, would make government an independent force in the exercise of power. They would, as we shall see, make the word *bureaucracy* a synonym for such independent exercise and for its presumed abuse.

6

No one looking at the role of ideas in defense of capitalism in the last century — and extending into this one — or at those in conflict with it can doubt their service either in support of the power of the capitalist system or in opposition. Ideas made the industrial capitalist seem the powerless and benign instrument of the market; in response, countervailing ideas made him seem the prime force in subduing and exploiting the worker. Thus the strength of social conditioning both on behalf of the power of high capitalism and in symmetrical reply. A question touched upon in the last chapter remains: to what extent was this social conditioning deliberately and artfully contrived? To what extent was it the product of men — Smith, Ricardo, Malthus, Bentham, Spencer, Marx, Engels — who truly believed they were dealing with the reality?

Overwhelmingly, it was the latter. No one, indeed, should suppose that effective social conditioning is always confined to those who believe what they say. In modern times the vast and costly public relations and advertising industry avows personal, business, and political virtue and pursues legislative and market needs in a spirit of forthright contrivance. Those lucratively involved would not dream of believing what they invent or avow. Contrivance is a business on which truth does not impinge. In more subtle fashion, scholars and publicists who deal in social interpretation and description take account of their audience, and assess the quality of their own ideas, by the extent and volume of the reputable applause.

It was not so of the great exponents of capitalist conditioning. Or of Marx. It cannot be imagined that the classical defenders of high capitalism wholly ignored the approval they evoked. Marx, a man of notably independent instinct, behavior, and thought, was certainly not indifferent to the response of workers or above adjusting his writing and speech to enhance that response. But the strongest defense of capitalism — the most powerful social conditioning — came from those who believed deeply in the analysis, description, and prescription they offered. It was the same with those who led the attack. Social conditioning did not originate with those skilled in contrivance. It came, initially, from those who thought themselves deeply in harmony with the truth.

XIV

The Age of Organization

THE SOCIAL CONDITIONING of high capitalism was
broad and deep. So was the countering response it en-
gendered. And both continue influential to this day. The
market remains to many the solvent of industrial power;
the modern corporation is still thought to be led as by an
invisible hand to what is socially the best. The Marxist ideas
are still a specter of evil — or hope. And herein lies one of
the problems of social conditioning as an instrument of
power: it is accepted as the reality by those who employ it,
but then, as underlying circumstances change, the conditioning does not. Since it is considered *the* reality, it conceals the new reality. So it is in the most recent great movement in the dynamics of power — the rise of organization
as a source of power and the concurrent lessening in the
comparative roles of personality and property. The older
vision of the economic order is still avowed, and for it policy
is still prescribed. Meanwhile a new order has arrived and
has the modern relevance. Over this the older social conditioning spreads a deep disguise.

The rise of organization in modern times is, for those

who are willing to see it, clearly visible. Its influence is felt in the economy, in the polity, and in the special and somber case of the military power; it manifests itself in a hundred forms of citizen and (as it is called) special-interest effort to win the submission of others, either directly or by way of the state. The management-controlled corporation, the trade union, the modern bureaucratic state, groups of farmers and oil producers working in close alliance with governments, trade associations, and lobbies — all are manifestations of the age of organization. All attest to a relative decline in the importance of both personality and, though in lesser measure, property as sources of power. And all signify a hugely increased reliance on social conditioning as an instrument for the enforcement of power. Property, as earlier observed, has much of its remaining importance as a source of power not in the submission it purchases directly but in the special conditioning by way of the media — television commercials, radio commercials, newspaper advertising, and the artistry of advertising agencies and public relations firms — for which it can pay.

2

The shift in the sources of power in the modern business enterprise is of the most striking clarity. The dominant personalities of high capitalism have disappeared. During the last century and into the present one, the names of the great entrepreneurs were synonymous with the American industrial scene. And the case was the same, if less dramatically so, in the other industrial countries. Now, outside the particular industry and not always therein, no one knows the name of the head of General Motors, Ford, Exxon, Du Pont, or the other large corporations. The power-

ful personality has been replaced by the management team;
the entrepreneur has yielded to the faceless organization
man. Thus the decline of personality as a source of power.

The role of property has similarly declined. In the age
of high capitalism none could doubt the power originating
in the ownership of capital. It was this property that accorded the right to run the business, and it was this that
gave access to influence in legislatures, over Presidents and
prime ministers, and with the public at large. Property as
a source of industrial power is not negligible now — as
ever in these matters there are no perfect cases — but it
has, nonetheless, suffered a major relative decline. The
thousand largest industrial enterprises in the United States,
all vast organizations, currently contribute about two thirds
of all private production of goods and services, and the
concentration of economic activity has followed a similar
course in the other industrial countries. In few of these
corporations and in none of the biggest does ownership by
the individual stockholder give access to authority within
the firm. This has long been so; it is fifty years since the
pioneering scholars Adolf A. Berle, Jr., and Gardiner C.
Means concluded that in the majority of the largest two
hundred corporations in the United States control had
passed to the management, which is to say the managers
elected the board of directors, which then, in an incestuous
way, selected the management that had selected them.[1]

[1] *The Modern Corporation and Private Property* (New York: Macmillan, 1933). The shift in power was further affirmed by the studies
of R. A. Gordon, among them *Business Leadership in the Large
Corporation* (Washington, D.C.: Brookings Institution, 1945), and
in the more general writings of James Burnham. See *The Managerial
Revolution* (New York: John Day, 1941). The bureaucratization of
modern economic enterprise was strongly emphasized by Joseph A.
Schumpeter — "it is an inevitable complement to modern economic
development" — in *Capitalism, Socialism, and Democracy*, 2nd ed.
(New York: Harper and Brothers, 1947), p. 206. It is obvious that

The continuing transfer of power from owners to managers — from property to organization — has been a pervasively characteristic feature of industrial development ever since.

Two factors contributed to the decline of property in relation to management. With the passage of time, ownership holdings in the enterprise were dispersed by inheritance, including, inevitably, to some heirs eminently disqualified by disposition or intelligence to exercise the power that property conferred. And, at the same time, the industrial tasks became increasingly complex. Corporate size, sophisticated technology, and the need for specialized management and marketing skills united to exclude from decision making those whose principal qualification was the ownership of the property. Power passed beyond the intellectual reach of the nonparticipant and thus beyond his or her capacity to intervene effectively. And increasingly within the enterprise, decisions emerged not from the single competence of any one individual but from the several contributions of specialists meeting in committee or close daily association.[2]

The decline of property in relation to organization as a source of power has not been accepted easily. A certain legitimacy is still thought to be attached to property. Its importance is affirmed by quasi-religious observances; the young are still told that *ultimate* power in the modern corporation rests with the stockholder. "When, for example,

---

the shift from property to organization as the prime source of power in the industrial enterprise is not a discovery of recent date. For a comprehensive contemporary treatment of this subject see Edward S. Herman, *Corporate Control, Corporate Power* (A Twentieth Century Fund Study) (Cambridge: Cambridge University Press, 1981).

[2] These are matters with which I have dealt in *The New Industrial State,* 3rd. ed. (Boston: Houghton Mifflin, 1978). C. Wright Mills made the point some twenty-five years ago: "Decision-making . . . at the top [of the corporation] is slowly being replaced by the worried-over efforts of committees, who judge ideas tossed before them, usually from below the top levels." (*The Power Elite* [New York: Oxford University Press, 1956], p. 134.)

John purchased a new issue of stock from the Keim Corporation last year . . . [it gave] him a voice in the decision of 'his' firm's management when he meets with other stockholders at annual meetings."[3] University faculties and students labor under the belief that, by the exercise of its vote in stockholders' meetings, their institution can substantially affect corporate decisions. At such yearly meetings a repetitively devout obeisance is accorded to property ownership; the obligatory reference, as indicated by the Department of Commerce pamphlet quoted above, is to "your company." No important management decisions are ever altered by any of these observances.[4]

3

With the shift in the sources of power from personality and property to organization went a marked diminution in the relative effectiveness of compensatory power and, as might be expected, a very great increase in the exercise of conditioned power. This was evident, among other places, in the relationship of the industrial firm to the union, of which earlier mention has been made. The trade union, as a countervailing exercise of power in the purchase of labor, had emerged before the age of organization. We have seen that it met with a far more adamant opposition from the early entrepreneurs — in the United States from Henry Clay

[3] From "Do You Know Your Economic ABC's? Profits in the American Economy," an instructional pamphlet on economics (Washington, D.C.: United States Department of Commerce, 1965), pp. 17–18.
[4] "[S]tockholders, though still politely called 'owners,' are passive. They have the right to receive only. The condition of their being is that they do not interfere in management. Neither in law nor, as a rule, in fact do they have that capacity." Adolf A. Berle, Jr., *Power Without Property: A New Development in American Political Economy* (New York: Harcourt, Brace, 1959), p. 74.

Frick, Henry Ford, and Sewell Avery[5] — than from the organization men. The property-owning industrialist was frequently interested in power for its own sake, in subduing the workers as an act of personal will and purpose; a vice president in charge of labor relations, on the other hand, is measured in part by his ability to keep the peace. And — a not insignificant point — he is not defending his own personal property from the aggressions of the workers. The age of organization[6] has thus brought a major easing of the compensatory power once exercised over the labor force.

When it came to the exercise of the same kind of power over consumers or customers, the change with the rise of organization was rather more subtle and, in some respects, contradictory in practical effect. Here, as with the employment of workers, power consists at its greatest in getting the most submission for the least cost. Much can be had for little if the buyer's need is great and if alternatives are not available; the consumer is exploited, as is the worker in the parallel case of submission. The classic example of such exercise of power is the monopoly of some essential or much-desired product for which there is no clear substitute; there being no alternative seller, the need and power are large. Competition enters as the remedy; hence its reputation as the basic solvent of power.

Organization and associated industrial development have had a marked, even profound, effect on both competition and monopoly. A major purpose of the great industrial enterprise, the labor union, the farm organization, the organization of petroleum-exporting states, or the professional

---

[5] Of Carnegie become United States Steel, the Ford Motor Company, and Montgomery Ward, respectively.

[6] Along, of course, with the effect of higher wages, unemployment compensation, and Social Security, all of which have widened the gap between condign and compensatory power and lowered the level of compulsion associated with the latter.

or trade association, is to restrain or eliminate price competition — to ensure, so far as may be possible, that there is no alternative at a lower price. In the case of modern industrial enterprises, this does not require formal communication; it is sufficient that there be a common understanding that price competition, if allowed to get out of hand, will be at cost to the power of all. Even the classical tradition in economics has come generally to concede the commitment to such implicit restraint — to what is called oligopoly pricing. Thus a primary purpose of organization has been to escape the power-limiting tendencies, otherwise called the discipline, of the market, and this has been widely successful.

But opposing influences have also been at work. The affluence associated with modern industrial development has greatly diminished the pressure of any given consumer need; the expansion in the number and variety of products and services has directly increased the alternatives available to the consumer. The choice among consumer products is infinitely greater than in the last century and therewith the sources of enjoyment and ostentation. Consequently, monopoly has ceased to be the ogre that it was in the earlier days of compensatory power. Those who might be subject to its force have the possibility now of buying something else or not buying at all. A little-noticed but highly significant result is that monopoly as a social ill has ceased, in recent times, to be an important subject of agitation in the industrial lands.

The consequence of this development has been a major shift from compensatory to conditioned power. One answer to the excessive availability of alternatives is to persuade people that they are not *real* alternatives — to cultivate the belief that the product or service in question has qualities that are unique. From this comes the massive modern commitment to commercial advertising. Advertising is not, as some would suggest, a new and vital form of market competition. Rather, it seeks through conditioned power to retain some of the authority over the buyer that was earlier associated with compensatory power.

The change here is evident in the symmetrical response of consumers to the power of sellers of goods and services. When they were subject to compensatory power — to the power that required of them much for little — they established cooperatives or buying associations to exercise a compensatory power of their own in return. These groups sought to buy more for less, developed alternative sources of supply, or appealed to the government to regulate prices or otherwise dissolve the market power of the seller. The price of the product, the index of relative compensatory power, was the central concern. This is so no longer. The preoccupation of the modern consumer is now all but exclusively with the advertising of the product, with countering the exercise of conditioned power in order to learn what is true or what is deemed to be true. This is also manifest in the actions of government agencies on behalf of the consumer. Prices are best an afterthought; central to all concern is the validity of advertising claims, what passes for truth in advertising. This is the modern purpose of the consumer movement; it is the predictable response to the passage from the exercise of compensatory power to the exercise of conditioned power.

4

When the modern industrial enterprise seeks support for its purposes from the state, conditioned power is again the instrument that it invokes or that is ultimately involved.

138

The forthright purchase of legislators and other public officials is not unknown; however, it is now regarded as offending the finer ethical sense, and, to a considerable extent, it has also been suppressed by law. The major exercise of power by the corporation over the legislator or public official is by cultivating belief in its needs or purposes either directly or in the constituency to which he is beholden. What is called a powerful lobby is one skilled in such direct conditioning or one that can appeal effectively to sizable responsive groups and associations and through them to their political representatives.[7] No one can suppose that pecuniary resources — property — are unimportant in this connection. However, they have their importance not in direct compensatory action but, as earlier noted, in the larger social conditioning they can buy, including that which may be used on behalf of a pliable or supportive legislator or against one who is adversely inclined.

The exercise of conditioned power in the modern state — the persuasion of legislators, public officials, or their constituencies — is no slight thing. It assails the eyes and ears and is a subject of major political comment and concern. However, it is probably not as efficient as the direct purchase, or compensatory power, that was commonplace in the era of high capitalism. Also, as we have already seen, compensatory power had its inescapable nexus with property, and property, in turn, was possessed in largest amount by the industrial capitalists. Conditioned power also requires pecuniary resources to pay for the diverse forms of persuasion — television, radio, and newspaper advertising, speeches, personal blandishment — on which it relies. But even granting this need, it is more generally available than the com-

[7] Thus in the United States the power for their own purposes of war veterans, people living on Social Security, and members of the National Rifle Association.

139

pensatory power it replaces. Resources can be found; money can be raised. In some measure, if often very slight, conditioned power is available to all who can form an organization.

5

Not only is conditioned power more widely available in the age of organization, but that available to the modern large corporation is, in some respects at least, weaker than the conditioned power associated with the pre-eminence of capital or property in the last century.

As massive organization manifested in the great industrial enterprise has become the basic fact of modern industrial life, the social conditioning on which its power extensively depends has not, as already noted, kept pace. Instead, it has remained basically unchanged from the age of classical capitalism. Power is still held to be dissolved by the market and by competition. And it is assumed that power, whatever its intention, is always guided to socially desirable ends by the miracle of the market and the competitive struggle therein. In consequence, the social conditioning of the last century is perpetuated in circumstances of increasing implausibility in the world of great organizations.

The continuing use of the earlier conditioning is vividly evident in economic instruction. The real world is one of great interacting organizations — corporations, unions, and the state. The interaction between union wage claims and corporate prices has become the principal modern cause of inflation. But a textbook that took as its point of departure the reality of such interaction would not be acceptable for college or university use, and, significantly, it would not lend itself to the geometrical and other mathematical refinements that are compatible with the assumption of market competition and without which the teaching of economics is not considered wholly reputable.

The social conditioning that is sustained by this instruction does have a certain effect. Hundreds of thousands of otherwise intelligent young people have their thoughts guided innocuously away from the exercise of industrial power. We have seen that power is served in many ways and that no service is more useful than the cultivation of the belief that it does not exist. "To recognize that microeconomics must now deal with a world of pervasive oligopoly . . . would threaten some basic ideological defences of the *laissez-faire* system."[8]

But social conditioning, however deep and pervasive, cannot collide too obviously with reality. The presence and power of the modern great corporations — Exxon, General Motors, Shell, Philips — are hidden only with increasing difficulty behind the market façade. In consequence, a reference to neoclassical economics, the conditioning medium of instruction, has come to have a vaguely pejorative sound; something no longer quite real is implied. Once economic instruction is perceived not as the reality but as the guidance away from the reality, its conditioning value is, not surprisingly, impaired.

The conflict with reality becomes greater when the classical social conditioning passes out of the field of education into everyday executive expression and the public relations and advertising effort of the large industrial firm. Then qualifications disappear; the power-dissolving role of the market becomes an absolute; Exxon is held to be indistinguishable from the corner grocery or the village pharmacy in its exercise of power. As a consequence, the persuasive

[8] Thomas Balogh, *The Irrelevance of Conventional Economics* (London: Weidenfeld and Nicolson, 1982), p. 60.

effect is confined to the unduly susceptible, those capable
of believing anything today, who, accordingly, will believe
something else tomorrow. For yet others an important effect
of the social conditioning of corporate propaganda, as significantly it is often called, is to cultivate disbelief. There
must be some misuse of power when those who so obviously
possess it are so at pains to deny having it. In the industrial
countries it is now a minor mark of sophistication that one
does not believe what one reads or hears in the public-
interest advertising of the great corporation. The conditioned
and compensatory power of the modern business enterprise
remains considerable, but it cannot be supposed that it
rivals the forthright compensatory power of the great
capitalist firm in the age of high capitalism.

There is a further indication of this decline in the relation of the modern corporation to the state. In the last
century, when the state was an ally, an adversary relationship between government and business would have been
unthinkable. Now government and business are widely regarded as mutual enemies. The social conditioning of the
modern corporate enterprise is extensively concerned with
the intrusive, limiting, and otherwise malign tendencies of
the state. (Only in the area of military power is there full
harmony between government and its dependent corporate
enterprises.) In important measure, the reason lies in the
shift from compensatory to conditioned power. Compensatory power was the clear monopoly of the business firm. The
legislators and public officials it purchased were not likely
to show hostility to their paymasters. Conditioned power
allows many more interests access to the state; some of
these are hostile to the business power and thus contribute
to the adversary relationship, seeming or real, between corporate enterprise and modern government.

But the state also has changed; in contrast with its role

in the last century, it is much less the instrument of those who seek its power, much more a power in its own right. Organization and conditioned power are again the operative forces. The modern state encompasses a large organization — bureaucracy — which, in turn, has made the state extensively the instrument of its own purposes.

XV

Organization and the State

IN THE NINETEENTH CENTURY and continuing some decades into the twentieth, the modern state was widely seen as the instrument of industrial capitalist power. On this Marx in the European revolutionary tradition and Thorstein Veblen and Lincoln Steffens in the American critical tradition wholly agreed. It was, as noted, an exaggeration; the state also reflected and served the diverse purposes of its citizens and of those who made up its structure. But all emphasis was on its service to industrial (and financial) interest.[1] Not until well into this century would anyone have thought of a conflict between government and industry, a commonplace expectation in our own day. There was also in the last century a certain exclusivity in the exercise of industrial power; both directly and through the state it was *the* power. Nothing rivaled the personality,

---

[1] "Despite its continuing preeminence and power, and its considerable influence over government, business has suffered a relative decline *from its pre-1930s position of almost exclusive domination of government policy.*" Edward S. Herman, *Corporate Control, Corporate Power* (A Twentieth Century Fund Study) (Cambridge: Cambridge University Press, 1981), p. 185. Italics added.

144

property, and organization of the industrialist in winning submission. This also is no longer true. A striking feature of the age of organization is the huge number of organized groups — trade unions, trade associations, political action committees, farm organizations — that seek to appropriate the instruments of power of the state for their own purposes. And also the greater number of organizations within the structure of the state itself — departments, agencies, authorities, public corporations, the armed services — that have become original sources of power. These two developments now merit attention.

2

The modern state unites within its structure all three sources of power — the political personality, property in the form of the resources it commands and dispenses, and organization. It has manifest access to all three instruments of enforcement: it remains, as suggested, the nearly sole possessor of condign power; it deploys large compensatory power; and it makes massive and growing use of conditioned power. All these sources and instruments of power were available in some measure in the last century and before. What has changed is their absolute and relative importance within the formal structure of government and the extent and diversity of their use by organizations outside the formal structure of government — organizations that seek to invoke the instruments of power of the state on their own behalf.

In considering the exercise of power through and by the modern state, it is useful, even necessary, to distinguish between the outer and inner orientations of the government and the mediating forces between them. The outer orientation is the legislature, the voters, and the great mass of organizations that bear on them and directly on the legislature itself. I shall refer to all these as the exterior processes of government. There is also the inner orientation — the continuing structure of government, in modern times a very large complex of organizations. These I shall refer to as the autonomous processes of government. They are broadly, although by no means wholly, coterminous with what is called the bureaucracy.[2] The pejorative connotation commonly attaching to that word expresses the feelings of many, including certain recent Presidents of the United States,[3] who are subject to or in conflict with its power. This must not, however, be taken to mean that the autonomous or bureaucratic exercise of power is socially inimical. On the contrary, it serves the highest of civilized purposes — protection of the people from hardship, exploitation, and abuse, that is, regulation of the exercise of condign power; support for their livelihood; support for industrial achievement and education; advancement of knowledge; encouragement of the arts; preservation of national resources; and hundreds of other functions. In speaking of autonomous or bureaucratic power, I do not pass judgment on its social merits.[4]

Standing between the autonomous and the exterior processes of government is, in many instances, an intermediary process — in the United States, the President, his acolytes and staff, the cabinet officers and their appointed subordinates. These exercise power and win submission to their

[2] The armed services are very much a part of the autonomous processes of government, but they are not usually embraced by the concept of the bureaucracy. I return to them in the next chapter.

[3] Presidents Carter and Reagan both eloquently assailed the large, mentally intractable and otherwise "horrible" federal bureaucracy. When John F. Kennedy was confronted with suggestions as to a seemingly wise course of action, he was sometimes disposed to reply, "I agree, but I don't think we can get the government to agree."

[4] Or, indeed, on its legitimacy, a central philosophical concern of many who write on power.

own purposes. But much of what appears, superficially, to be an exercise of their power is, in practice, a mediation between autonomous and exterior claimants on power.[5]

I turn first to the exterior processes of government.

3

It was extremely useful to the exercise of the industrial power to have the public believe that all effective power was dissolved by the subordination of the industrial firm to the market. We have seen that the effort to instill this belief survives strongly in economic instruction. A similar design operates regarding the power of the government. Nothing better conceals the exercise of power in and through the state than the political litany, undertaken virtually as a form of religious office, that all men and women come equally in their sovereignty to the polling place and are subject to the result in accordance with the will of the majority. This the young are told; this the truly good citizen accepts. And this the daily practice openly, visibly, comprehensively denies. In the last century the democratic liturgy concealed, though far from effectively, the purchase of voters, the purchase of those for whom the people voted, and the compensatory power over voting explicit in the use of patronage. By all such means the votes of the many were gathered to the purposes of the few. In the present century the liturgy conceals a more imaginative subversion of the democratic electoral process. The voter is still held to be sovereign; the sovereignty of the majority is still converted to the purposes of the few. The difference in

[5] There is a more formal depiction of these power relationships in Dennis H. Wrong, *Power: Its Forms, Bases and Uses* (New York: Harper Colophon Books, 1980), pp. 158 et seq.

the age of organization is that there are a great number of highly competitive organizations engaged in the effort to subordinate the voter and his or her elected representatives to their purposes, and the dominant instrument is now conditioned power. Corporations, the weapons industry, business enterprises generally, trade unions, farm organizations, religious institutions, consumer groups, and a near infinity of organizations with other more specialized purposes now participate routinely in the exterior processes of government and seek to win the submission of voters on behalf of their own needs or goals. Or they seek the submission of those already elected. Property and the associated compensatory power are highly important in the exterior processes. But in all but the most deviant cases they do not reward the voter or those elected; rather, they pay for the social conditioning that has become the effective instrument of power.

In the modern state, and notably in the United States, this social conditioning is exercised with the greatest intensity. Speeches, newspaper publicity and advertising, radio and, above all, television commercials, are of central importance in the modern political campaign. The volume and strategy in the use of these instruments for winning belief — for conditioned power — are thought decisive. As important as the candidate himself or herself is the person who is presumed to possess the talent and knowledge for the management of the requisite social conditioning.[6]

As expected, the exercise of conditioned power in the exterior processes of government brings a symmetrical re-

---

[6] For a wide-ranging, impressive, although somewhat unstructured, discussion of the modern role of money in politics, see Henry Bretton, *The Power of Money* (Albany: State University of New York Press, 1980), pp. 164 et seq. A very recent and compelling account is in Elizabeth Drew's *Politics and Money* (New York: Macmillan, 1983).

148

sponse from those resisting it. This is a greatly evident phenomenon in the modern state. Those who organize and seek to persuade voters and legislators on the evils of abortion are countered by those who organize to persuade on the right of women to free choice. The organization and persuasion of those who seek reductions of, or exemptions from, taxes — who urge the need for incentives to induce their own investment or effort — are countered by those who organize and persuade on the need to close tax loopholes. Those who would have prayer in public schools encounter those who would confine it to the churches and the home or forgo its benefits.

Because organization and conditioned power as its means of enforcement are so readily available in the exterior processes of government, they are greatly used. The sheer volume of the effort has, in turn, a profound effect on the efficiency of this instrument. So liberally is it wielded — in direct persuasion, through the media, by speeches, books, pamphlets, and in other ways — that voters and legislators develop an immunity to what the mind cannot conceivably absorb. That so much exercise of conditioned power has little or no practical effect — wins slight or no submission — does not, however, lessen its use. It is uniquely available. Also, all who engage in it have an impression of their own power — they have held a meeting, made a speech, appeared on television, produced a commercial, published a book, written an article or an editorial; accordingly, they must have exercised power. The action is the surrogate for the result; resort to an instrument of power is widely confused in our time with an exercise of power. To this, an aspect of the illusion of power, I will return.

4

Central to the conditioned power of the organizations operating in the exterior processes of government are the further principles of organization as outlined in chapters VI and VII. Specifically, if the organization seeking submission to its purposes is internally strong — if its members submit completely — then its ability to win external submission, in the present case the submission of voters and legislators, is proportionately greater. And the fewer the purposes the organization pursues and for which it requires submission, the greater its internal discipline will be. Great power is exercised by the National Rifle Association among voters and legislators in the United States. This reflects the narrowness of its objective — the preservation or legalization of the right to possess and, presumptively, to use lethal weapons. In like manner, organizations in opposition to or in support of women's rights, affirmative action programs, and the so-called right-to-work laws have a similar discipline and a similar singleness of purpose. This is recognized in everyday practice in the respect that is accorded the single-interest or special-interest lobby. It may be noted in this connection that the power of conservative organizations in the exterior processes of government is likely always to be greater in proportion to the number of their participants than that of liberal organizations. Thus organizations opposing women's rights and abortion, though repeatedly shown to be less numerous in the electorate as a whole, have, at least in the past, proved themselves to be stronger in legislative effect. The reason is the greater conservative instinct for discipline. The conservative mood accepts the established beliefs, the social conditioning; the liberal instinct is to question, challenge, and debate.

5

The autonomous processes of the state comprise the many, varied, and frequently very large organizations that administer the tasks of modern government. In the United States the departments, agencies, bureaus, commissions, and authorities, along with the armed forces, make up the permanent structure of the government. These organizations owe little to personality as a source of power; it is a measure of its slight importance that their members are regularly referred to as faceless bureaucrats. They owe more to property — to the considerable and sometimes very large resources they possess and deploy.[7] But most of all, the source of their power lies in extensive, complex, and, in the most important cases, disciplined organization.

It is a marked feature of the autonomous processes of government that they have access to all three of the instruments of power. In varying degree and subject to the further control of the courts, they have access to condign power; they have extensive access to compensatory power; they rely heavily on both implicit and explicit exercises of conditioned power. A reference to a government of limited powers, a

---

[7] The limitation on the exercise of compensatory power, or rather on the financial resources that support it (that is, the control of appropriations), is the major instrument of power of the exterior processes of government vis-à-vis the autonomous processes. While the focus of all interest, it is not a uniquely powerful instrument. The autonomous units of government, after some central review and adjustment, propose their budgets to the legislature, and in all but the more routine instances their requests are met.

common characterization of the government of the United States, refers almost always, it may be noted, to condign power. No similar moral and legal restraint is placed on the rather more important exercises of compensatory and conditioned power.

In the autonomous processes of government conditioned power is, again, of primary importance. A powerful agency of government, though it ordinarily has access to compensatory reward and may have access to condign punishment, will rely in greatest measure on conditioned power. Implicit conditioning — a general acceptance of the purposes of the particular agency — is supported by a major flow of information on those purposes by way of meetings, speeches, and coverage by press, radio, and television. Also frequently involved is a sophisticated management of what is made available to the public. In the United States government the Department of Defense, the Central Intelligence Agency, the Department of State, and the National Security Council all give, as a matter of routine, the most careful attention to what is so released; it is taken for granted that such information and the hoped-for belief will serve the best interests of the agency in question. Material in conflict with the purposes of the agency is routinely withheld; not infrequently it is made subject to classification, which is to say its unauthorized release will result in the threat or reality of condign action. Nothing is thought more damaging — bureaucratically more reprehensible — than "unauthorized" leaks. The associated discussion and controversy over managed news, leaks, and classification reflect the importance attached to social conditioning as a source of power. Journalists and others rightly sense that a major instrument in the exercise of power is involved. Agencies of the United States government that have no capacity to manage information — the Departments of Commerce, Labor, and Agriculture —

have no power comparable with those that have such control.

The ability to handle information successfully is an aspect of the larger discipline that relates the internal to the external power of organization. The public agency that extracts from its members a large measure of submission to its purposes includes in that submission the surrender of their freedom of expression. This is one vital aspect of a more general submission, which, in the extreme but by no means exceptional case, means the abandonment of independent thought to whatever reflects the goals of the organization. It is then that one is known as a good soldier, a good public employee, a good "agency man," a good foreign service officer, a person who "really believes" in what he is doing. When this subordination is complete and reliable, the agency in question is proportionately stronger; when the subordination is slight or lacking, it is predictably weaker.

The conditioned power of the autonomous processes of government is also greatly enhanced by the size and complexity of the tasks of the modern state. This complexity removes its purposes from easy public comprehension and thus from the effective response of those whose submission is sought. And it will regularly be avowed that its purposes are too complicated for the untutored to understand; cultivation of the belief that this is so then becomes an aspect of social conditioning. In past times much of the power of the U.S. State Department, as also of its counterparts in other countries, rested on the belief that foreign policy was too subtle and intricate a matter for the average citizen or the ordinary politician to comprehend. Outsiders should keep out, not challenge the power of those who had a monopoly of the requisite knowledge and skills. The same social conditioning technique is now employed with great effect by those concerned with weapons policy and arms control, as the next chapter will tell. This deliberate conditioning, in combination with the size, complexity, and technological and other sophistication in the tasks of modern government, leads to the submission that is evident in the phrase "We must leave it to the experts."

Finally, power in the autonomous processes of government depends on their direct relationship with organizations in the exterior processes and the associated and cooperative exercise of conditioned power. The extreme case is the Department of Defense in alliance with the weapons firms. But many and perhaps most of the autonomous agencies of government have companionate organizations in the exterior processes — the Department of Agriculture and the farm groups; the Department of State and, as it is called, the foreign policy establishment; the Bureau of Land Management of the Department of the Interior and the cattlemen whose livestock graze the publicly owned lands; the Army Corps of Engineers and those who ply the waterways.

Where the exercise of power by the autonomous processes of government is adverse to the purposes of organizations and individuals in the exterior processes, the dialectic of power also operates. A nuclear freeze movement develops to counter the lethal preoccupations of the Department of Defense and the weapons industry; conservationists rally to the protection of federally owned wildernesses; environmentalists organize to counter an unduly relaxed attitude on toxic-waste disposal. As ever, the exercise of power invites a generally symmetrical response.

In considering the autonomous processes of government, one is led to emphasize the role of organization and its associated social conditioning as the dominant manifestations of power. However, as in all these matters, there are no absolutes. What is called a powerful bureaucracy will have access to the other two instruments of enforcement, and these will derive from all three sources of power. Thus, in its years of prominence, the Federal Bureau of Investigation was rightly considered a powerful agency. In J. Edgar Hoover, it had at its head an unquestionably effective personality. It was generously endowed by the Congress with money — property. And it owed some of its power to a highly disciplined organization — the full submission to the purposes of the Bureau of those who served in its ranks. Turning to the instruments of enforcement, it had access to condign power both within the framework of law and through the unpleasant extralegal consequences it could invoke for those who resisted or criticized its methods. From its revenues it had adequate, even generous, compensatory power for those who served its purposes. And careful attention was given to social conditioning, to cultivating belief in the virtuous aims and high effectiveness of the organization and the deep depravity of the subversives and criminals with whom it contended and from whom it provided protection. The consequence of this combination of sources and instruments of power was an aggregate of power that, for a long time, no President thought it wise to challenge. But eventually here too there was an answering dialectic. The power of the FBI aroused opposition and was substantially curtailed.

6

Between and in some measure over the autonomous and the exterior processes of the modern state is, as noted, a combination of executive and mediating power; in the case of the United States, this is the President and his coterie of appointed officials. The President, needless to say, is an original source of power. The office also reflects — and fully — the modern trends in the exercise of power. Personality remains of undoubted importance, although it is considerably less decisive than is commonly advertised and imagined. The resources that the President has at his command — the role of property — are a major source of power. And here, as elsewhere in modern times, organization is of greatly increased significance. The President is now the creature of a very large inner personal administrative staff; some seventy-nine men and women currently surround and assist him in his tasks. Up until the time of Franklin D. Roosevelt, there was little such supporting organization in the White House; Woodrow Wilson wrote his speeches himself on his own typewriter.

With respect to the instruments of power, recourse to condign power is, of course, closely circumscribed. It is not considered appropriate or even lawful that the Chief Executive should have discretion in decisions to prosecute crime, and certainly not in the penalties imposed. The compensatory power of the President is great; directly or indirectly the resources that he deploys — those that he can offer or withhold — win a generous measure of submission. The desirability of this reward and the thought of its possible loss are suitably in the minds of a very large number of people. This compensatory power extends down to frivolous details — attendance at the social observances of the White House and the bestowal on the ostentatiously faithful of minor presidential souvenirs or honors.

However, the modern President increasingly and inevitably relies most upon conditioned power. It is to this that the White House organization accords major, nearly exclusive, concern; it is to this end that its discipline is extensively directed. The closest attention is paid, as a matter of high urgency, to press conferences, speeches, other public appearances, indeed, to all association with the media. Any significant need to win submission by extending power over the exterior processes of government — the organizations seeking power from the state, the voting public — leads more or less automatically to a presidential address on television. As in the autonomous processes of government, it is considered of the utmost importance that the release of information in conflict with the required social conditioning be controlled or suppressed.[8]

7

Although the original power of the presidency is considerable, there could conceivably be more error in exaggerating than in minimizing it. A very large part of what superficially appears to be presidential power is, as we've seen, the mediation between conflicting exercises of power — between those of different parts of the autonomous processes of government or between the autonomous and the exterior processes of government. This mediating power should not be thought a small thing. But what results from its exercise is not the original will of the President or his staff but that of one or another (or in partial measure of both) of the contending organizations.

Other factors give an enhanced impression of presidential power. Because the traditional association of power is with personality and the person of the President is greatly

[8] In the administration of Richard Nixon, this led to the (eventually) widely publicized operations of the so-called plumbers and the equally notorious wiretapping of staff members. Both reflected the concern for preventing the release of information damaging to the required belief. The grounds for complaint against both of those exercises of power were, however, not the effort to control the release of information — that was taken for granted — but rather the particular techniques of suppression.

evident, he and his office are assumed, in accordance with all conventional thought (or the absence of it), to have much power. Those who write of presidential power are deeply subject to this syllogism.

There is also the matter of the illusion of power, a factor that has been greatly enhanced by the modern reliance on social conditioning. Since the submission won by any exercise of conditioned power is subjective and relatively invisible — in contrast with the far more objective results of the exercise of condign or compensatory power — there is, as already mentioned, a strong tendency for the submission to be taken for granted. If the President makes a television address or promulgates a new weapons policy or pleads for support for his budget, a generally favorable response to the presidential purpose is assumed; the exercise again becomes the result.

The illusion of power is also heightened by those who are close to the presidency. Presidential acolytes are particularly enthusiastic in its exercise; by emphasizing the power of the Chief Executive, they, *pari passu*, enhance their own in the public eye, and this, in turn, becomes a compelling contribution to self-esteem. The exaggeration effect comes even more strongly from the journalists, television reporters, and other media specialists who work in close association with the White House. All deeply participate in the exercise of conditioned power — their reporting contributes indispensably to the needed belief and, on occasion, to countering it. This participation gives an enhanced sense of power to which all but the least susceptible are dangerously subject.[9]

[9] Television and newspaper reporters covering the White House have a strong impression of the grave responsibility, which is to say power, they possess. It is the intention of nearly all so employed to write a book on the authority thus exercised. And in any given year several do. None of these works minimizes or makes light of the exec-

8

None of this is to argue that the illusion of power in the various processes of government outweighs the reality. There are manifestations of the power of the state where the reality is very great indeed — where, among other things, the conditioning is so deep that even a calm discussion of the power involved can be subject to the reproach that one is not fully in harmony with the national interest. This is true of the military power, a formidable and, as I have said, somber exercise of power, which is the subject of the next chapter.

---

utive power to which the author is occupationally adjacent. And on few subjects is an author so secure against criticism. In the nature of conditioned power there is no way of distinguishing the reality from the illusion. And the author is safe against any charge that he may be exaggerating his power, for his critics will be his colleagues, who will be equally persuaded.

XVI

The Military Power

THERE IS A SUCCESSFUL expression of power when the individual submits to the purposes of others not only willingly but with a sense of attendant virtue. The supreme expression, of course, is when the person does not know that he or she is being controlled. This, at the highest level, is the achievement of conditioned power; belief makes submission not a conscious act of will but a normal, natural manifestation of the approved behavior. Those who do not submit are deviant. To a marked degree in our time such submission is the achievement of the military establishment, by far the most powerful of the autonomous processes of government. Support for a strong national defense is an expression of normal patriotism; no truly good citizen dissents. This highly successful conditioning is, however, only part of an even larger manifestation of power. The power of the military embraces not only the significant sources of power but, with extraordinary comprehensiveness and effect, all the instruments of its enforcement. It is an awe-inspiring thing, not made less so by its potential, even probable, consequences.

None of this is to say that the power of the military has

escaped attention; more than any other exercise of power in our time it is the subject of grave public unease. And of symmetrical resistance. We are now in a position to see that this concern is, in fact, justified. We must hope that from a clearer view of the sources of its strength will come a stronger design for countering its power.

2

Of the three sources of power, the military establishment has two in large amount — property (which is to say financial resources) and organization. In the past, and notably in wartime, personality was also important. As late as World War II in the United States, Britain, and Germany, there were impressive leaders — George C. Marshall, Dwight D. Eisenhower, Douglas MacArthur (already a highly visible figure in peacetime), Bernard Montgomery, and Erwin Rommel. Where personality did not exist, it was extensively synthesized with the less-than-reluctant help of the press. But in the modern military establishment personality has little significance. In the Vietnam War the generals involved, despite considerable effort to the contrary, were both forgettable and quickly forgotten.[1] This is even more the case with those who now serve in positions of formal authority in the armed forces. Hardly anyone outside the Pentagon knows the names of the present Joint Chiefs of Staff. Here, as elsewhere in the age of organization, personality as a source of power has given way to the anonymous organization men.[2]

[1] Reporters covering military campaigns are, in the usual case, peculiarly at the behest of the generals they cover. It was one of the decisive weaknesses of the military power in Vietnam that it lost control of the press.

[2] The effort to synthesize personality has continued in modern

From the sources of military power in the vast resources it possesses and deploys and in its huge, institutionally disciplined organization, there proceeds, in turn, a not unimportant access to condign power and a comprehensive submission won by both compensatory and conditioned power.

Little need be said about the property resources of the military establishment. In the United States they far exceed any similar source of power;[3] they embrace not only what is available to the armed services and the civilian military establishment but what flows out to the weapons industries and the large investment in plant and working capital these sustain. From this wealth comes the compensatory power that wins the submission of soldiers, sailors, and airmen, the huge civilian roster of the Department of Defense, and the employees, executives, and owners of the weapons and other ordnance firms.

The compensatory power deriving from the property resources of the military — the submission won from both its own personnel and its suppliers — is there for all to observe. But because it is so visible, there has been some error of emphasis in identifying the true locus of the military power. In the seemingly sophisticated tradition that associates power with industrial enterprise — in reality, a holdover of Marxist thought and the dominant critical atti-

---

times in the case of Secretaries of Defense. All, while in office, are thought to have certain marked personal traits that give them power, but, as earlier observed, the power of those traits does not survive a return to private life.

[3] "The Department of Defense employs more people and spends more money on the purchase of goods and services than all the rest of the government put together. The Department of Health and Human Services has a larger budget, but that budget consists almost entirely of transfer payments to individuals." Adam Yarmolinsky, *Governance of the U.S. Military Establishment* (New York: Aspen Institute for Humanistic Studies, 1982), p. 1.

tudes of the last century — military power is extensively assumed to be associated with the defense industries. The military industrialists are the deus ex machina; they both procure and profit from the military budget. There is no doubt that the power thus exercised is great: the submission of scientists, engineers, executives, workers, and the defense-dependent communities is won thereby. Of this power legislators are made acutely conscious, and campaign contributions from the corporations involved add to their awareness. In such fashion the compensatory power of the military enters and in some degree dominates the exterior processes of government.[4] However, the relative visibility of the defense industries and their obvious connection with the exterior processes of government should not lead anyone to minimize the other institutions exercising military power. The defense industries are an extension of a larger structure, the heart of which lies in the autonomous processes of government — in popular parlance, the Pentagon. And important as are compensatory power and its source in property or financial resources, the more important instrument of the military power is conditioned power with its intimate relationship to organization.

---

[4] Enforcing at a minimum a discreet silence. Commenting on the reluctance of business executives to express active concern over the threat of nuclear war and annihilation, Robert Schmidt, vice chairman of the Control Data Corporation and president of the American Committee on East/West Accord, has observed, "A lot of business people choose not to raise their profile by getting into that kind of discussion," noting that it does not give them any "points with the government or the administration." And William Alden of the Alden Computer Systems Corporation has said that many business leaders are unwilling to take a stand because they fear the Pentagon might "blackball" their companies. Quoted by Florence Graves in "Are These Men Soviet Dupes?", *Common Cause* (January/February 1983).

3

In much of life a certain merit is thought to be attached to independent self-expression. This, in turn, is hostile to tight, disciplined organization with its symmetrical relationship to external power. The strong conditioning of military organization, both that of the armed services and that of the civilian establishment, is based, as we have seen, not in self-expression but in discipline. This is then reinforced by compensatory reward and condign penalty. The soldier who accepts fully the purposes of the organization gets promoted and is accorded a variety of honorific rewards. The recalcitrant is subject to condign punishment, including dishonorable expulsion or, at the extreme, court-martial. Such condign power is uniquely possible in support of military discipline; it is not elsewhere available in public or private organization.

Discipline is less strong in the civilian component of the autonomous processes of the government and specifically that part associated with the military. However, the employees of the Pentagon are not noted for speech or action in conflict with the purposes of their organization. The one who openly dissents faces the perilous prospects of the whistle blower. And there are, as in all organizations, many ways of suppressing lesser dissidence. Promotion is denied; the individual ceases to participate in collegial action; he is no longer thought responsible or reliable; he becomes unacceptable as an associate in social observances. The force thus compelling discipline is very great; nothing is more damaging to the military power than a public impression of internal discord and conflict.[5] This internal discipline then becomes the counterpart of strong external effect, as we saw in chapters VI and VII.

4

An essential, indeed vital, need for the conditioned power of the military is a specific enemy. If the military power is to be more than traditional, ceremonial, or precautionary in character, a hostile threat is indispensable. Such a threat wins the appropriations — the property — from which compensatory power derives. It also leads to consolidation of belief within the military establishment and similar belief outside. Internal discipline must be kept tight; external dissent or opposition must be subject to the suspicion or assertion that those involved are aiding, abetting, or motivated by the enemy.[6] At a minimum they are unpatriotic; at most their dissidence verges on treason, invoking the traditional threat of condign punishment. Deeply conditioned attitudes affirm the value of patriotism, and these become of absolute importance when there is external danger.

In the period since World War II, North Korea, China, North Vietnam, and pre-eminently the Soviet Union have served the United States as the enemy threat. Years of a mildly relaxed relationship with the U.S.S.R. in the 1970s were visibly damaging to the American military power. The abandonment of détente after 1980 coincided, by no means

[5] As when, in 1982, it became known that a majority of the Joint Chiefs of Staff were opposed to the so-called dense-pack basing of the MX missile.

[6] In the early 1980s, it was said that advocates of a freeze on nuclear weapons were being manipulated by the Soviet Union or were otherwise subservient to its purposes.

accidentally, with a large increase in military expenditures. The former was clearly necessary to allow of the latter.

Related to the existence of an enemy are the control of information and the resulting social conditioning. The need to keep military secrets from the enemy justifies preventing complete access to the general public. What is then released can be substantially and even extensively what best serves the needed public belief — the required social conditioning. This includes the military's view of enemy intentions and particularly of what is needed in the way of weaponry. Critical discussion of ordnance and weapons systems is made subject to the restraints of classification — as well as those generally of organizational discipline — and to the condign punishment or its threat that defends against the release of classified material. The military power, in its management and control of information, is, by a wide margin, the most comprehensive and successful exponent of conditioned power.

Not that this exercise of power is unchallenged. As the last chapter stressed, continuing and sharp controversy surrounds the management of information in the interests of national security. What control is appropriate, necessary, and justified? What is inappropriate and self-serving, an improper exercise of the power to classify? Again controversy rightly underlines the importance of this control — this service to conditioned power — in the modern exercise of military power. All who welcome restraints on power should cherish and encourage this continuing dispute.

5

Not all the control of information by the military power is the result either of the discipline of organization or of formal controls. Much is the result of the sheer size of the organization involved and of the technical character, real or avowed, of the issues. The citizen looking at the mass and complexity of modern military technology surrenders to those who are presumed to have mastery. Or he surrenders to surrogates who are thought to be in command of the requisite detail. And he is strongly encouraged to do so. The consequence is an argument between experts from which the public is excluded, with the effect that the social conditioning of the military power is effectively unchallenged in the civilian world.

A highly important case of this exclusion by technical complexity is the arms-control issue. In recent times this has been the nearly exclusive possession of the arms-control specialists. They, in turn, are a small community technically accomplished in the weaponry involved, jealous of their presumed knowledge of Soviet weapons and intentions, and theologically adjusted to the concept of mass death. With no slight indignation they exclude the intervention of outsiders. What can doctors, bishops, or untutored professors know about such complicated matters? What entitles them to speak or interfere? The self-confident convictions of the arms-control theologians are the supreme expression of conditioned power. Almost casually the nuclear arms community assumes and defends power to arbitrate and control not only questions of individual life and death but the question of the survival of the human race. Of all the expressions of power cited in these pages this one is transcendent, for inherent in its exercise is the power to end all other exercises of power.

In the United States, as in other democracies, it is thought wise and even necessary that the military power be kept subordinate to civilian authority and restraint. This is a well-established point of law. It is also a restraint that is questionably effective in practice. In nearly all recent Pentagon confrontations, when faced with the strongly conditioned attitudes of the military establishment, civilians have surrendered thereto. They wish to be thought forthright, decisive, heroic, and otherwise in keeping with the conditioned military virtue. They must show that they can master the intricacies of military operations and of weaponry, that they are no less aware than soldiers of the need for military defense. In consequence, many civilians — on the National Security Council, frequently in the State Department, in the intelligence agencies, and notably in the Department of Defense itself — have ended up being more warlike, more committed to weapons systems and large budgets, than the members of the armed forces themselves.

6

Great though it is, the military power is not plenary. The purposes it pursues are not inherently attractive. Death that is no longer confined to junior officers and enlisted men[7] but is now, prospectively, a mass civilian experience does not lend itself naturally to conditioned power; nor does enforced military service. The Vietnam War produced in the United States one of the most comprehensive efforts in social conditioning in modern times. Nothing was spared in the attempt to make the war seem necessary and acceptable to the American public. The effort failed when countered by an

[7] High-ranking officers having long since escaped this threat. "The nearest the modern general or admiral comes to a small-arms encounter of any sort is at a duck hunt in the company of corporation executives at the retreat of Continental Motors, Inc." C. Wright Mills, *The Power Elite* (New York: Oxford University Press, 1956), p. 189.

even larger and more pervasive dialectic.[8] Eventually it was accepted that military operations could no longer be sustained in the face of, as it was said, an increasingly hostile public opinion. The military power overreached its resources in conditioned power; the result was a substantial reverse. Now, a decade later, there continues to be the publicly expressed hope that Vietnam has been forgotten. That, in the present terminology, is to express the wish that the social conditioning that was then so adverse to the military power is no longer operative.

As this is written, there is indication of a similar dialectic based on compelling current circumstances. The modern militiary power in the United States is strongly committed to nuclear weapons, a commitment that has led to extensive conditioning on their necessity and even their benignity. This, in turn, has had the predictable symmetrical reaction, a leading manifestation of which has been the nationwide demand for a freeze on the development, deployment, and testing of those weapons. And there has been a yet larger effort both here and in Europe to urge negotiation of effective control and reductions of all armaments in an atmosphere of relaxed political and military tension. This challenges the need of the military power for an enemy and allows for and encourages the possibility of a similar move-

---

[8] The dialectic became especially strong as the draft — the prospect of military discipline and the possibility of death — reached those in the college and university community who had a capacity for self-expression and a resulting ability to find an audience and make their objections known — that is, to engage in social conditioning on the unwisdom of the war. The draft involves the substitution of condign for compensatory power to induce military service — to win submission to the military power. It is not, as this is written, publicly acceptable in the United States, although it survives in other countries, including such committedly neutral lands as Austria and Finland.

ment in the Soviet Union. It seems proper to ask, in face of the current military power, that all who read these pages involve themselves with this countervailing effort. On its effective use human survival itself can depend.[9]

[9] Reference in these pages has been to the miltary power in the United States. This power has a general counterpart in the other industrial countries and, needless to say, in the Soviet Union. However, it is in the new (and some older) nations of Asia, Africa, and Latin America that it has its most comprehensive role. Of a total of 134 independent states in the world no fewer than 39 are now, by an acceptable calculation, governed by military dictatorships. The power so expressed is a varying combination of the sources and instruments here identified. Personalities emerge, though often of a dim or even repellent sort. Armies command and deploy substantial property resources from the public treasury, and, above all, in a world where it is exceptional and exiguous, they have organization. (Latin American armies are not models of rigorous and effective discipline, but in most of these countries no other organizational structure rivals them in this regard.) From the resources commanded by the military establishment comes compensatory power over its soldiers — a very effective expression of power in the poor rural society where military service is a major upward step in economic well-being. There is a substantial, if not always compelling, exercise of conditioned power, much of it concerned with benefits in conflict with military purpose. Most important of all, there is a generous availability of condign power for suppressing dissent both within and outside the military organization. The result is that military power has become the major threat to civilian and democratic process the world around.

170

XVII

The Power of Religion
and the Press

IN MODERN TIMES both the sources and the instruments of religious power in the Christian world have greatly diminished. The power once deriving from a divine presence — from personality — still exists; there is widespread deference paid to it every day. But as even the most devout will agree, the vision has dimmed as compared with the earlier perception of it. For many the holy presence is invoked only as a Sabbath-day routine or under conditions of extreme personal necessity or terror. And by some it is wholly resisted and denied.

The power of personality is still present in certain contemporary religious leaders — in the United States the Reverend Billy Graham, the Reverend Jerry Falwell, the Reverend Oral Roberts, the Reverend Sun Myung Moon, and numerous less notable figures of, however, marked local effect. They are hardly to be compared with the great religious voices of the past. A strong public instinct also confines the modern preacher or priest to, in the main, religious themes. Those who step beyond to seek submission on sexual practices or the sanctity of private enterprise are commonly thought to be extending their activities in an undue way.

The property of the Church has also declined greatly in relative importance as a source of power. Once of magnificent extent, it is now of minor magnitude when compared to secular resources. The wealth of the Vatican commands respect for its mystery and possible misuse rather than for its size.

Finally and most dramatically, there has been the dissolution of organization. What was once the internally (and relatively) disciplined and monolithic organization of Christianity by the Catholic Church has now become hundreds of diverse and, in most cases, loosely structured groups, each in some measure of competition with all the others.

2

With the relative and absolute decline in the sources of power has gone a similar but much more damaging weakening of the instruments of enforcement. Condign punishment for living Christians is no longer permissible; and, as earlier observed, its use as a threat for the hereafter has also greatly diminished. To cite fear of eternal punishment as a reason for avoiding unacceptable behavior or thought while still alive (that is, for submitting to the authority of the Church) is at least mildly old-fashioned.

Compensatory power — the purchase of religious conformance — has disappeared as well. The promise of heavenly reward remains for many a substantial incentive to submission, but it is far less powerful than in the past. The evanescent character of this promise as compared with earthly compensation is evident in the reproving statement "He will have to get his reward in Heaven."

Until well into the present century, the specific care and feeding of the needy both at home and abroad was a not unimportant design for obtaining their religious obedience. Those so enticed regularly regarded the church observances and requisite submission as the price they had to pay for food, shelter, and medical succor. Compensatory power in the form of hospital care and schooling was used to win submission in primitive societies, and it extended, on occasion, to outright purchase. Such exercise of compensatory power is now of negligible importance in the undeveloped lands, and in the industrial countries it has been extensively replaced by the welfare apparatus of the modern state.

In consequence of the foregoing, conditioned power remains almost the sole reliable means for winning religious submission. It is of undoubted effect, but it too has suffered. From the Middle Ages until well into the present century, as previously indicated, the power of religion owed much to its near-monopoly of access to conditioned enforcement. No other voice spoke with similar authority even on secular matters, and dissenting opinions were silenced by forms of condign action that could be exceptionally definitive. Now the exercise of conditioned power in all modern communities is profoundly competitive.

Basic to the earlier virtual monopoly of that power by religion was its control of education. The secularization of the school system was, therefore, a major blow, one resisted to this day both by the Catholic Church, with its continued commitment to its own educational establishment, and, in attenuated fashion, by those who seek prayer and other religious observances in the public schools.

Science has also made deep inroads on the erstwhile

religious monopoly. Of this little more need be said, for almost nothing has been left unsaid. Scientific conditioning is also a powerful instrument. It derives from the occasional significant personality, from important property resources that accrue to its support, and from substantial organization. As a manifestation of conditioned power, the conditioning of science is, on the whole, far more rigorous and far more disciplined than that of modern religion. The religious mind is thought to be pliable and diverse; the scientific mind is a precise, strictly channeled instrument. Religious observances are loosely structured; scientific procedures have rigid parameters. Science and religion operate in an uneasy association, protected by the frequent comment that there is no irreconcilable conflict between the two. No one should be misled; the effect of science on the religious power, specifically on its conditioned power, has been enormous. There may be an exception in the case of the Fundamentalist sects, where science inconsistent with the doctrine, notably the Darwinist system, is righteously excluded. This is an exception that demonstrates the rule.

Where once there was only one source of religious conditioning, that of the local priest, now there are many voices from many churches. Once also the priest, in his weekly adjuration, had a near monopoly of access to the public mind; as late as the last century only books (for the few to whom they were available) and the local newspapers were his rivals in this area. Now the most devout communicant returns from the Sunday service to turn on television. That and radio, newspapers, magazines, political speeches, and books are now all readily available and in competition with religion for public attention. It is not without significance that the religious figures of greatest influence in our time are those who have most successfully exploited the resources of radio and television.

The implicit as distinct from the explicit conditioning of religion remains considerable. It continues to command a greater measure of submission to the broad canons of religious doctrine than we may, in fact, know. But both the implicit and explicit conditioning of religious authority are subject to the mass competitive cacophony that is part of the contemporary exercise of conditioned power. Both, in consequence, have diminished in significance, as have the other sources and instruments of the power of religion.[1]

[1] The reasons for the decline in religious authority in the Christian Church become clear when Christian power is contrasted with the greater continuing power of other traditions, notably that of Islam. For Moslems personality remains much more important; it is manifested by the stronger presence of both God and the Prophet and by prayers for their intercession, which play a highly prominent role in the daily routine. Physically extant personalities, such as the Ayatollah Khomeini, are far more significant. And Islamic organization has a far greater internal discipline and consequent external effect. It is, indeed, weakened by the divisions between the two great convocations, the Sunnis and the Shiites and the rivalry and even hatred between the two, but organization, nonetheless, remains a much stronger source of power than that available in the even more deeply divided Christian tradition.

It is in the instruments of power, however, that Islam has its greatest strength. Condign power is still exercised with great effect, both in this world and as promised for the next. Deviation can be subject to an exceptionally sanguinary set of punishments, extending in extreme cases to amputation or, in the case of noncompliant women, death by stoning. Of the eventual fate of nonbelievers no one is left in doubt.

Complementing the condign enforcement is a far more vigorous exercise of conditioned power than is known in the Christian world. The Quran, the revelations of Allah to Mohammed, does not allow of liberal discussion. The *suras* are the word of law; the truly devout know many by heart. Also Moslems, defending the conditioning power of the Quran and the religious power in general, rightly see or sense the dangers of competitive Westernized communication — of the intruding and seductive effect of newspapers, radio, television, and Western secular and scientific attitudes. To the extent that these are successfully resisted, the discipline of the Quran and the religious authority of Islam are further enhanced.

3

The power of the press and of radio and television derives, as does that of religion, from organization; its principal instrument of enforcement, like that of religion, is belief — social conditioning. At one time, personality was important; it was exemplified in the United States by the great press lords, as, significantly, they were called — Adolph S. Ochs, Joseph Pulitzer, William Randolph Hearst, Colonel Robert Rutherford McCormick — and in Britain by Lords Rothermere and Beaverbrook.[2] So also in broadcasting, with David Sarnoff and William Paley in the United States and Lord Reith in Britain. Now, overcoming some effort to the contrary, the heads of the great newspapers and broadcasting networks are largely anonymous. Encountered at social gatherings, they must, like the president of IBM, introduce themselves; when presenting checks, they are asked for identification. In the press and on television names and faces abound, but much of this is synthetic personality, created by organization for the purposes of the organization. It reflects not the real but the traditional role of personality. In television much of the information that is passed on to the public has emerged from the organization, not from the individual; on occasion, the person who reads it has not seen it except for a brief rehearsal. In all cases, the reporter, anchorman, or commentator speaks from within the framework of the organization; all are subject to organizational attention and constraint, even though this may be denied in moments of self-appreciation. On major newspapers the columnist who consistently advocated his or her personal

[2] Rupert Murdoch, it will be suggested, continues in this tradition. This, perhaps unfortunately, is true.

176

preference for the death penalty, a massive and effective curb on the military power, or free abortion would be regarded with some discomfort. The great personalities of the press in the past saw their papers as instruments for persuasion; they did not dream of according space for the opposing view. In the modern press and television it is taken for granted that any strong opinion must be balanced by another in careful opposition.

Property remains important for the press and television; its compensatory power is what sustains the large and expensive structures involved. But organization is, once more, the decisive source of power. It is the social conditioning flowing from organization and determined by the character of organization that sustains and wins the external submission.

This submission is, undoubtedly, great. The belief that was once accorded the priest — and perhaps in lesser measure the schoolmaster — is now accorded the spokesmen and -women of television and the press. Allusion to the source of belief is universal and automatic — "I read it in the paper" or "I saw it on television." It is with reference to some press or television comment that nearly all political conversation begins; it is with the effect on public belief of such news or analysis that a very large part of all political discussion is concerned. In combination with property, the persuasive power of television is subject to a measure of financial calculation. Once the chances of candidates for public office were appraised in accordance with personality or policy; now the commonplace calculation turns on the comparative amounts of money they will be able to collect for television advertising.

4

Yet there is more danger of overestimating than of under-
estimating the power of the modern media. There are, as
noted, the constraints imposed by organization as a source
of power. Since an organizational judgment is collective, it
obviates individual deeply and persistently held positions.[3]
Beliefs must be balanced with appropriate countervailing
beliefs. None of this produces the conditioning that emerged
in times past from strongly articulated, much reiterated
personal advocacy.

A yet more important reason for reservation as to the
power of the modern media — of television and radio, as
well as the press — is the volume of the current persuasive
effort. This, it need hardly be emphasized, is huge. It is
inevitable, in consequence, that given the limitations of the
human mind and memory, much is ignored and more is
promptly forgotten. Enduring belief is not won, and only a
random effect is achieved from whatever belief is temporarily created. What captures some evades others. The lesson for religion applies. Its conditioning was powerful when
it was simple, uncluttered by doubt or dissenting view, and
when it had a monopoly of access to the human mind. So
with the modern press and broadcasting media.

It was earlier observed in the case of the politician that
after telling an audience what it wishes to hear and listening
to the resulting applause, he regularly associates his recep-

---

[3] During political campaigns television networks and stations do
not seek, in any serious way, to influence the election of candidates,
the vote on referenda, or public attitudes on issues. Overwhelmingly,
their comment is on who is ahead, who is behind, and what tactics
are winning or losing votes. For television an election campaign is a
species of spectator sport. This, too, reflects organizational constraint.

178

tion with successful persuasion. This is an important case
of the illusion of power, and the same illusion operates
strongly with the media. Reading or hearing what they already believe, readers and listeners make known their favorable reaction. This, in turn, is taken to be influence. It is so
regarded even when the initial communication was written
or televised with a specific view to eliciting such approval.
Indeed, in the extreme case, the television station or network
ascertains by research what the viewer most wants to hear
and see, responds to that desire, and then accepts that the
viewer response is the result of its persuasion.

Finally, influence — the achievement of belief — is reduced by the overt improbability of much that is urged. This
is especially so of television. Commercials on the high
therapeutic powers of commonplace medicinal preparations,
the social gains from whiter clothing, the avowed moral tone
of aspiring politicians, all invite a compelling disbelief. Since
this is the tendency regarding some of what is seen and
heard, there is a tendency to disbelieve all.

What *has* been successful as regards the power of the
press and television has been the persuasion as to that power,
a belief that extends inevitably to the participants themselves. The point has previously been made. The self-esteem
of the Washington reporter or network commentator is ad-
mirably served by meditation on the power he or she exercises. The sense of this power is then reflected not only in a
solemnity of mien but in much equally sober public writing
and confession, and it is further enhanced by the attention
and the efforts at social and like subornation of reporters,
editors, columnists, and commentators by politicians, lobbyists, and professionally righteous citizens who seek access to
the media.

Adding further to the impression of the media's power is
its role as a form of relief from political frustration. The

responsive and articulate citizen in our time sees much of which he or she disapproves. As there is some resulting resort to organization and speechmaking, so there is a resort to the media. Articles are written; letters are sent to editors; at a higher level, television interviews are welcomed. From all this comes a measure of psychic relief — something has been accomplished. Essential to this sense of accomplishment is a belief in the power of the media.[4]

Finally, there is what may be called the residual effect. Condign enforcement of submission has greatly declined in the modern industrial society. So, with higher levels of affluence, has the strength of the compulsion associated with compensatory power. The pressure of need is less; the alternatives are greatly more numerous. What remains is conditioned power. To this the press and television have an obvious relationship. It must, accordingly, be the true modern expression of power. What else is there?

No one should minimize the power of the media; in organization and social conditioning it combines the great modern source and the great modern instrument of power. Nonetheless, the power of the press and television must be seen in careful perspective. That includes the possibility that the general exercise of all power has declined — that, as compared with earlier times, there is now much less submission of some to the purposes of others. It is in the context of this general decline that the exercises of power that remain — that of the modern military establishment and, more generally, those of the state and the great corporate enterprises — must be viewed.

---

[4] Implicit in Marshall McLuhan's famous chapter title "The Medium Is the Message." (*Understanding Media: The Extensions of Man* [New York: McGraw-Hill Paperback Edition, 1965], pp. 7–21.)

XVIII

A Final Word

The Concentration and Diffusion of Power

IN THE MIDDLE AGES there could have been little talk or thought of power. It was massively possessed only by the prince, the baron, and the priest. For the citizenry in general, submission to it was natural, automatic, and complete. Except as husbands might enforce it on wives and elders on children, it was not something that the ordinary individual ever expected to exercise. Nor, after the rise of capitalism, was the situation much changed. There was still government and religious authority, and now there was the power of the merchant and the industrialist. The laborer who went daily to the mill submitted nearly the whole or his or her life to the command of the owner; what little remained was controlled by the state and the Church. The notion of some independent area of authority did not arise. For the silent masses, powerlessness was the natural order of things. Power was not discussed because only a tiny minority of people exercised it. The singular (and to many, the damaging) achievement of Marx was in persuading the working masses that this lack of power — this submission — was not natural or inevitable. Power could, in fact, be gained.

Power is a compelling topic today not necessarily because it is more effectively exercised than before but because infinitely more people now have access to either the fact of power or, more important, the illusion of its exercise. The modern reality is a combination of great organizational concentrations of power and great diffusion among individuals in its exercise or seeming exercise. It would be convenient for present purposes were it one or the other, but, as ever, social reality exists as an admixture.

The concentration is clearly a part of the contemporary scene and will invoke only slight dispute; it is evident in the modern industrial enterprise, the modern state, and, combining and calling on both of the others, the modern military power. The concentration of industrial power can be seen in the mere handful of huge organizations that now dominate modern economic activity — the thousand or so that, as previously told, contribute two thirds of privately produced product in the United States and a similar concentration in the other industrial countries. This is in overwhelming contrast to the wide distribution of economic activity in the earlier age of market capitalism, including in the United States, and to the still widely distributed agricultural enterprises. The only thing that now disguises this concentration of economic power (and then not well) is the increasingly obsolescent conditioning that asserts the continued power-dissolving subordination of the firm to the classical market.

There is also, in contrast with earlier times, the massive apparatus of the modern state and therein, as we have seen, the modern military power. The latter — let there be no doubt — reflects a major centralization of power, with its access to all three of the instruments of enforcement and with strength deriving from two of the sources, namely the massive deployment of property and, by modern standards, a uniquely controlled and disciplined organization. That so many react so strongly, even so passionately, in its support is only a measure of the compensatory and conditioned power it commands. The aggregate of the power so exercised should never be dismissed from the more available mind.

2

As we have sufficiently seen, organization and the associated role of social conditioning are basic to all modern exercise of power. At the same time, and paradoxically, they bring not only the modern concentration of power but also its *personal* diffusion.

There is diffusion to participants within the structure of organization, notably within the modern corporation and the modern public agency, and even more there is the illusion of individuals in these organizations that they have and are using power. As personality gives way to organization, there is, inevitably, a wider participation in the exercise of power. What once expressed the will of the boss is now the product of bureaucracy — of conference and committee and proposals passing up through the organizational hierarchy for modification, amendment, and ratification. In the older business enterprise submission was to the owner; his word, as it was said, was law. In the modern large corporation submission is to the bureaucratic processes in which many participate. The boss, as he may still be called, is the agent of those who instruct him; the power he is presumed to exercise is at least partly the endowment of those who, sensitive to his vanity, attribute to him an authority that, were it real, would be disastrous. The modern corporate title expresses the reality: the chief executive officer — the CEO — is only the chief among those with executive authority. As with the modern corporation, so with the public agency. It, too, concentrates power and then distributes it among the individual participants.

There is proof of this internal diffusion of power when the top command changes in the great organization. Rarely in the modern business enterprise and not usually in the public agency is it expected that policy and action will much change as a result. It is accepted in practice, as distinct from the economic and political liturgy, that in great organizations power is exercised from within the management and not by the transitory figure at the top.

Within the organization the reality of personally exercised power consists in the ability, on occasion, to influence the purposes of the organization and to affect or contribute to the external submission that it seeks. So long as the individual submits to the purposes of the corporation or the public bureaucracy — submits to its internal power —he retains some capacity to influence its exercise of power. He or she is an influential executive or bureau chief, a hard-nosed foreman or supervisor.

Much more important, however, is the illusion. Some of this arises, once again, from the ostentatious deference that subordinates in an organization accord those above them in the hierarchy.[1] More important, perhaps, since the organization has power, the individual feels that some share of it is his own. His submission to the organization is complete, but by some subjective process of sharing, some of its power belongs to him.

---

[1] Including the Washington official who presents his superior, in the frequent case the President himself, with policy proposals for which there is no acceptable alternative and then compliments his principal on the wisdom of his choice.

The more marked manifestation of organization, however, is in combining a great concentration of power with a great multiplication of organized groups and great diffusion of power as between organizations. This latter leads on, in turn, to an even more comprehensive illusion as to its exercise.

3

The chief characteristic of organization is its constant and widespread availability. Compelling personality is in fixed supply, and this remains true even in a time when personality is extensively synthesized in politics and by the media. Property is also, at any given moment, in fixed amount. Organization, in contrast, is subject to unlimited proliferation. And as it is open to anyone to form an organization to advance his or her purposes, so anyone or any such organization can resort to the associated instruments of conditioned power. Speeches, pamphlets and books, television and other advertising, press releases, magazine articles, and a near infinity of other forms of persuasion are available. These are the modern manifestations of power; the resulting diffusion will be evident. So, and even more significantly, will be the illusion to which this form of exercise gives rise. By forming an organization, issuing statements, having access to television, people can believe they have power. All this, to stress once more, is the reason for the intense discussion of power in modern times. It is not because it is exercised with any special strength or because any great submission is won; such manifestations are far less comprehensive than in past times. It is because so many individuals have some power or the illusion of its exercise.

Life in all modern industrial societies, but notably in the United States, is distinguished by the number of organiza-

tions in competition for the public and political mind —
lobbies, political-action committees, public-interest organizations, trade associations, trade unions, public relations firms,
political and diverse other consultants, radio and television
evangelists, and more, ad infinitum. A common reaction,
often one of grave concern, is to their power. A more valid
perception is of the distribution or dissemination of power
that they reflect. Were power strongly concentrated in the
state, they would not exist. There would be no further power
to seek and share. It is because they are able to influence the
government and appropriate some part of its power that they
have function. This, in turn, is to say that the power normally associated with the modern state is also diffused.

4

Contributing further to the diffusion of power has been the
effect of affluence. This has weakened the role of property
and therewith of compensatory power. With affluence, consumers and workers have alternatives; it is less necessary,
accordingly, that they submit to any given exercise of authority. The needy consumer is subject to the power of the
landlord, shopkeeper, loan shark; the affluent one is not.
Monopoly is a source of power in a poor society; in a rich
country it invites people to find alternatives. The poor and
hungry worker submits to his employer; the well-paid employee is under a lesser measure of compulsion.

The compulsion is also weakened if there is income available in the form of unemployment compensation or welfare
payments as the alternative to hunger and hardship. As
earlier observed, no complaint is more common in the modern industrial society than that workers are no longer as
diligent and as disciplined as in the past. This complaint

should be directed, in part, against the affluence that has diminished the compensatory power of the employer. But it runs also against the Social Security and other benefits that have gone far to eliminate fear. Those who attack the welfare apparatus of the modern state correctly sense its role in diminishing and diffusing the compensatory power that, in past times, served employer power. Whether this is unfortunate, unwise, or socially deleterious is, to be sure, another question.

Power is also now diffused by its dialectic, of which sufficient has been said. Those who once accepted compulsion now organize automatically to resist it. This was not as true in earlier times; such a response was then regarded as subversive, an attitude from which those now exercising power are also not immune.

There remain, however, the great exceptions. The modern military establishment strongly concentrates power. It exacts a high level of submission from a large number of individuals within the organization, and in symmetrical fashion it exacts an equivalent obedience outside. The modern large corporation expects and receives a high level of conformity from the many in its management. And its property resources accord it an extensive command over the many it employs. From this flows an extensive submission by the citizenry and by the state. As in the case of the military, the purposes of the great business enterprise, the ideas that sustain it, are largely, though not quite completely, above debate. As social conditioning adverse to the military is unpatriotic and negligent of national security, so that which is adverse to the modern industrial enterprise is subversive of the free enterprise system. Not the least of the strengths of the military and corporate power is the diffusion in the sources of power that are brought in opposition. And also the *illusion* of power in the opposing dialectic. Nothing so serves the military or corporate power as the belief of its opponents that they have accomplished something by holding a meeting, giving a speech, or issuing a manifesto. No one in a democracy should be in doubt as to the real effectiveness of organized opposition to concentrated power. But all must have an acute understanding of the weakness arising from the diffusion of power and the difference between illusion and practical effect.

5

It is not the purpose of this book to pass judgment on the exercise of power, the notably alarming role of the modern military power apart. (The latter is not something of which one can take a wholly detached and analytical view.) There can be suffering, indignity, and unhappiness from the exercise of power. There can, as well, be suffering, indignity, and unhappiness from the absence of its exercise. Instead it is my hope that the reader will emerge from these pages with a reasonably solid sense of the nature and structure of power — of its sources and the instruments by which it is exercised, of the varied associations between the sources and the instruments of power, of their change over time, and of their modern form and effect. I would especially hope that there might be a better understanding of the great modern role of conditioned power, that power which is principally effective because we are so extensively innocent of its exercise — because we think of ourselves as responding to seemingly normal belief, seemingly natural and accepted virtue. I would also hope, needless to say, for a better perception of the illusion of power to which so many are subject and, as just observed, of the weakness in dealing with great concentrations of power that arises from the modern tendency to its diffusion in the countering exercise. Let us, where corporate or military power is exercised, recognize that effective consolidation of the countering power, not diffusion and competition as between many opposing organizations, is a major, indeed absolute, essential. Finally and more generally, I naturally hope for an enduring sense of what and how much lies back of our daily references to power and our equally constant involvement therewith.

INDEX

Index

Exploitation: of workers, 109; of consumer, 136. *See also* Condign power; Consumer(s); Labor
Exxon Corporation, 132, 141

Falwell, Reverend Jerry, 2, 69n, 171
Familial/parental power, 29, 34, 35. *See also* Children, submission of
Farm organizations, *see* Special interest (single-issue) groups
Federal Bureau of Investigation, 155
Federal Trade Commission Act, 126
Feudalism, 90, 93-97, 98, 99-100, 102, 109
Finland, 168n
First Amendment, 85-86
First International, 40, 121
Fogel, Robert W., 12n
Ford, Henry, 76, 136
Ford Motor Company, 76, 132, 135n
Foreign policy, 32, 41, 153, 154
France, 92, 98, 99, 103, 114, 119n
Freedom: welfare measures and, 51; vs. dictatorship, 67; of speech and expression, 85, 86, 153; of trade, 112 (*see also* Trade)
Frick, Henry Clay, 75, 114, 135-36
Fugger, Jakob 99n
Fundamentalism, 174. *See also* Religious power

Gandhi, Mohandas K., 39, 79-80, 86n
General Motors Corporation, 76, 132, 141
Germany, 2, 36, 66, 83, 114, 119n; in World War II, 61, 67, 161

Girdler, Tom, 76
Goebbels, Joseph Paul, 36, 66
Gordon, R. A., 133n
Gould, Jay, 114
Government, *see* State, the
Graham, Reverend Billy, 2, 171
Graves, Florence, 163n
Great Britain, *see* Britain

Hargreaves, James, 107
Harriman, E. H., 114
Hastings, Warren, 105
Hazlitt, William, 10
Health and Human Services, U.S. Department of, 162n
Hearst, William Randolph, 176
Hedonism, 117-18
Hercules, 39
Heresy/dissent, *see* Religious power
Herman, Edward S., 134n, 144n
Hill, Frank Ernest, 76n
Hitler, Adolf, 41, 66, 77, 84
Hobbes, Thomas, 24
Hoover, J. Edgar, 155
Hudson's Bay Company, 104

Incentive, *see* Compensatory power
Income, 6, 51. *See also* Property (wealth)
India, 105; British rule in, 58, 59, 79-80, 86n, 94; feudalism in, 94, 96
Indoctrination, 62. *See also* Conditioning, social (belief)
Industrial Revolution, 98, 101, 107, 108, 110
Industry, *see* Capitalism; Corporate or industrial power; Corporation(s); Special-interest (single-issue) groups
Inequality, economic, 116, 118. *See also* Economics
Inflation, *see* Economics
Information, *see* Media
Innocent III (pope), 92

Steffens, Lincoln, 144
Steuart, Sir James, 103
Strikes, 20, 57–58, 75–77. *See
also* Labor
Submission to power: conceal-
ment/nonrecognition of, 3, 6,
12–13, 70, 158, 160 (*see also*
Power); relationship to threat
and reward, 4–5, 17, 22–23;
awareness of, 5, 14; belief
(social conditioning) and, 5, 7,
23, 26, 27, 29, 35, 59, 70, 153;
education and, 5–6, 25, 32, 34;
organization and, 8–9, 12, 55–
56, 57–64, 65, 67, 68–69, 71,
93, 95, 101, 142, 150, 153, 164–
65, 170n, 175n, 183, 184, 187;
inevitability of, 13; difference
in nature and extent of, 16n;
by women, 20, 21, 23, 25–26,
82, 181; by children, 23, 32,
34, 35, 39, 82, 181; purchase
of, by leaders or groups, 28,
46, 49, 50, 52–53, 84–85, 139,
156 (*see also* Compensatory
power); media and, 31, 177;
religious authority or will, 33,
34, 35, 45, 46, 93, 172–73, 175,
181; personality and, 40–41,
44; of constituency, by "leader,"
45; property (wealth) and, 49,
53, 100, 132; military, 55–61
passim, 161n, 162–63, 168,
170n, 187; industrial capitalism and, 108–9, 110, 116, (U.S.
view of) 125; of elected officials, 148; military service
(draft) as, 169n; decline in,
180; acceptance of, 181–82.
See also Conditioning, social
(belief); Response to power;
Slavery
Sumner, William Graham, 117
Sunday, Reverend Billy, 2
Symmetry: bimodal, of organization (internal and external
submission to power), *see*

Organization(s); in response
to power, *see* Response to
power

Taft, Philip, 75n
Tawney, R. H., 102–3n
Television, *see* Media
Texas State Board of Education,
24
Tolstoy, Leo, 59
Totalitarian regime, 36–37, 65–
67. *See also* Dictatorship;
State, the
Trade: discovery of America
and, 100n, 105; competition
and, 101, 112, 113, 123, 126,
127, 136–41 *passim*; regulations and sanctions on, 101,
103–4, 107, 126–27, (removal
of) 112; religion and, 102n;
monopoly and, 104, 113, 126,
136, 137, 186, (legislation
against) 126–27; free, 119n.
See also Capitalism; Economics
Trade unions and associations,
18, 51, 132, 136, 186; differing
perceptions of, 11–12; sources
of power of, 46, 77; internal
and external submission by,
57–58, 64; response to power
of and by, 73, 81–82, 108,
125–26, 135, (labor conflicts)
20, 75–77; interaction of, with
corporations, 140. *See also*
Special-interest (single-issue)
groups
Trujillo, Rafael, 36, 83

Uganda, 83
Ulmer, Melville J., 8n
Unemployment, 122. *See also*
Labor
Unemployment compensation,
see Social insurance